W9-BEU-376

The People's Bible

Thessalonians

David P. Kuske

NORTHWESTERN PUBLISHING HOUSE
Milwaukee, Wisconsin

Second edition,   2000
Fifth printing,   1996
Fourth printing,   1990
Third printing,   1989
Second printing, 1985

Cover art by Frank Ordaz.
Interior illustrations by Glenn Myers.
Maps by Dr. John Lawrenz.

Covers of first edition volumes and certain second edition volumes
feature illustrations by James Tissot (1836–1902).

Library of Congress Card 84-60327
Northwestern Publishing House
1250 N. 113th St., Milwaukee, WI 53226-3284
© 1984 by Northwestern Publishing House.
Published 1984
Printed in the United States of America
ISBN 0-8100-1196-4

CONTENTS

The apostle Paul

EDITOR'S PREFACE

The People's Bible is just what the name implies—a Bible for the people. It includes the complete text of the Holy Scriptures in the popular New International Version. The commentary following the Scripture sections contains personal applications as well as historical background and explanations of the text.

The authors of The People's Bible are men of scholarship and practical insight, gained from years of experience in the teaching and preaching ministries. They have tried to avoid the technical jargon that limits so many commentary series to professional Bible scholars.

The most important feature of these books is that they are Christ-centered. Speaking of the Old Testament Scriptures, Jesus himself declared, "These are the Scriptures that testify about me" (John 5:39). Each volume of The People's Bible directs our attention to Jesus Christ. He is the center of the entire Bible. He is our only Savior.

The commentaries also have maps, illustrations, and archaeological information when appropriate. All the books include running heads to direct the reader to the passage he is looking for.

This commentary series was initiated by the Commission on Christian Literature of the Wisconsin Evangelical Lutheran Synod.

It is our prayer that this endeavor may continue as it began. We dedicate these volumes to the glory of God and to the good of his people.

INTRODUCTION TO 1 THESSALONIANS

The city of Thessalonica

Where was Thessalonica? What kind of city was it? If you had lived in the Roman Empire at the time when this letter was written, you would have known something about Thessalonica as surely as most Americans know at least a few things about Chicago and St. Louis.

Thessalonica was a large and important city of the Roman Empire. It had a population close to two hundred thousand. It was a leading city of the Roman province of Macedonia and thus a place in which Roman officials lived. Most important, it was located at a strategic point in the middle of the Roman Empire.

Like Chicago or St. Louis, it was a crossroad city. The Via Egnatia, the main highway from Rome to the east, passed through Thessalonica. Travelers would pass under the huge arched gates at the east and west city limits where this busy road entered and then left Thessalonica.

This highway had been built by the Romans for military purposes. They wanted to be able to move troops quickly from one part of their empire to another. A city such as Thessalonica, which commanded one of the most important points on this vital road, was of obvious strategic value to Rome.

Not only was Thessalonica an important land route city. It was also a major sea trade center of the Roman Empire. Since it was quite dangerous to sail around the southern shore of Greece because of the weather and rough seas, most goods shipped by boat from east to west went through either

Corinth or Thessalonica. At Corinth small boats would be rolled across the isthmus and then launched again, or the goods would be unloaded from a boat and hauled the few miles overland to another boat sailing for Rome or other points west. At Thessalonica, such goods would be unloaded from boats and then carted overland on the highway to the west.

Since Thessalonica had a fine harbor, it also became a naval station with extensive docks for the Roman navy. From this station, together with ports at Corinth and Ephesus, the Roman navy maintained a firm grip on the Aegean Sea, the body of water that was the vital hub of much of the sea trade and travel at that time.

As a large trade center, Thessalonica naturally was filled with people from all parts of the Roman Empire. Still, the major portion of the population would have been composed of native Macedonians. Many of these people worshiped the Greek gods whose "home," according to Greek mythology, was supposedly located on nearby Mount Olympus.

We can only begin to imagine what this thriving city was like: the overland carts and travelers streaming through its gates; the cargo-filled boats either anchoring or lifting anchor in its busy harbor; its streets filled with native shoppers, with Roman officials and military personnel, with Greek and Jewish merchants; and no doubt there was an undesirable person or two attracted by the excitement and temptations of a large city.

In this great city, the gospel took root as a result of Saint Paul's missionary activity. And it was to the flock in Thessalonica that Paul addressed two inspired letters.

Occasion and purpose

What led Paul to write this first letter to the Thessalonians? That question is best answered by reading the letter itself. Yet it will also help a great deal to review some of the background that we find in the book of Acts.

Some 20 years after Jesus' death, resurrection, and ascension, Paul began his second mission journey. About A.D. 51, God guided Paul and his missionary companions Silas, Timothy, and Luke to cross over from Troas in Asia Minor to Macedonia. You may remember the vision described in Acts 16:9,10 that we often refer to as the Macedonian call: "During the night Paul had a vision of a man of Macedonia standing and begging him, 'Come over to Macedonia and help us.' After Paul had seen the vision, we got ready at once to leave for Macedonia."

All of Paul's mission work in Macedonia was marred by one thing—fierce persecution. In Philippi, Paul healed a demon-possessed slave girl, and her owners had Paul and Silas beaten and jailed.

When Paul's preaching in the synagogue in Thessalonica brought significant success after only three weeks, the Jews became jealous and instigated a riot. This forced Paul and Silas to leave for Berea. When the Jews from Thessalonica heard that Paul was in Berea, they sent agitators there. So Paul left Berea and went on to Athens, while Silas and Timothy stayed behind in Berea. All this is recorded in Acts chapter 17.

Jewish opposition to Christianity was especially fierce in Thessalonica. Paul worried about how the congregation would stand up under the constant pressure of these determined Jews. It is not surprising, then, that when Timothy and Silas joined Paul in Athens, he immediately sent Timothy back to Thessalonica to encourage and strengthen the young Christian congregation there.

Later Timothy returned with a report. This report brought joy to Paul's heart because it contained good news about the Thessalonians. Not only had they remained faithful,

3

but in the very face of the Jewish persecution, they were actively spreading the gospel from the city of Thessalonica into all of Macedonia!

Relief combined with joy moved Paul to write a letter to the Thessalonians. He wanted them to know how thankful he was for the faithfulness that God's Word had produced in them. He also wanted to add to the encouragement Timothy had given them in his visit.

So it was that late in the year 51 or early in 52, the apostle addressed this letter to his beloved Thessalonians. This early date makes 1 Thessalonians one of the first, if not the very first, of Paul's letters. Only Galatians may have been written earlier.

Author

At first glance it might seem that there are three authors of this book, namely, Paul and Silas and Timothy. All three are mentioned in the address of the first verse. Throughout most of the letter the plural—we, us, our—is used.

There are, however, a number of places in which the singular *I* is used. For example, in 2:18 Paul states, "We wanted to come to you—certainly I, Paul, did." This indicates that the real author of the letter is Paul himself.

He uses the plural throughout most of the letter to indicate that everything he writes is shared by Silas and Timothy. These two men had taken part with Paul in founding this congregation. Timothy had been Paul's personal agent sent to strengthen and encourage them. The Thessalonians would have no trouble understanding why Paul would include Silas and Timothy as joining him in all he said in this letter.

Summary

Paul spends roughly the first half of the letter (1:1–3:9) expressing his love and concern for his fellow Christians in

Thessalonica. He opens with a prayer of thanksgiving that God had worked both perseverance and an active mission zeal in them. Then he reviews for them his ministry in Thessalonica not for purposes of self-glorification but to confirm the point that he had not come to get something from them like so many traveling teachers in that day. Rather, he came to share the treasure of God's Word with them. In the final section of the first half of the letter, he tells the Thessalonians why he had sent Timothy to them and how Timothy's report had brought him joy and renewed his zeal for the work in Corinth.

In the second half of the letter (3:10–5:28), Paul does what he also hoped to do when he saw them again face-to-face. By a series of encouragements, admonitions, and instructions, he supplies what is still lacking in their faith. He reviews God's will in regard to sex and marriage. He exhorts them to brotherly love. He urges them to be ready at all times for Christ's second coming. He exhorts them to honor their spiritual leaders, practice Christian love, and, finally, pattern their whole lives after God's will.

In this letter Paul speaks of the Thessalonians as a "model to all the believers in Macedonia and Achaia" (1:7). At the same time the Holy Spirit guided him to build up their faith where necessary.

That same Holy Spirit also has seen fit to have these words preserved for us to read. There is much that we too can gain from this sacred epistle.

Outline

   A. God's Word produces faithfulness (1:1-10)
      1. Thanksgiving for the Thessalonians' faith (1:1-3)
      2. God's Word works a firm faith (1:4,5a)
      3. The Thessalonians' faithfulness—a model for others (1:5b-10)

B. The work of a faithful pastor (2:1-12)
  1. He is bold in the face of opposition (2:1,2)
  2. He looks on his work as a sacred trust (2:3,4)
  3. He is as unselfish as a gentle mother (2:5-7)
  4. He is an untiring worker (2:8,9)
  5. He is like a father caring for his children (2:10-12)
C. Faithful endurance in persecution (2:13–3:9)
  1. God's Word works faithfulness in persecution (2:13-15a)
  2. The Jews opposed God's Word to their own condemnation (2:15b,16)
  3. Paul sent Timothy to strengthen the Thessalonians (2:17–3:3a)
  4. Paul feared for their faith (3:3b-5)
  5. Timothy's report gave Paul great joy (3:6-9)
D. Living to please God (3:10–4:12)
  1. Paul prays that God may increase their faith and love (3:10-13)
  2. Paul urges them to live by his instructions (4:1,2)
  3. God's will for sex and marriage (4:3-8)
  4. Being led by brotherly love (4:9-12)
E. The coming of the Lord (4:13–5:11)
  1. Believers who have died will not be left behind when Christ comes (4:13-15)
  2. Encouraging one another with the resurrection (4:16-18)
  3. Christ's coming will be a disaster for many (5:1-3)
  4. Christians are to put on God's spiritual gifts (5:4-8)
  5. A reminder of why Jesus died (5:9-11)
F. Final instructions (5:12-28)
  1. Hold spiritual leaders in high regard (5:12,13)
  2. Practice Christian love (5:14,15)
  3. Pattern your whole life after God's will (5:16-22)
  4. Closing prayer, greeting, benediction (5:23-28)

PART ONE

God's Word Produces Faithfulness
(1:1-10)

Thanksgiving for the Thessalonians' faith

1 **Paul, Silas and Timothy,**
To the church of the Thessalonians in God the Father and the Lord Jesus Christ: Grace and peace to you.

Paul begins this letter in the way in which most letters were written at his time. First, he states from whom the letter comes. Next, he indicates to whom the letter is written. Then, he follows with a greeting.

How could Paul describe the Thessalonians as being "in God the Father and the Lord Jesus Christ"? Paul knew the Thessalonians were being tested by persecution, but he also knew they continued to remain faithful. The Thessalonians did not have a mere outward connection with the Father, but they were truly in God. Their suffering had drawn them closer than ever to their heavenly Father and the Lord Jesus Christ.

The name *Lord Jesus Christ* tells us three things about God's Son. *Lord* reminds us that he is the true God to whom we belong and whom we serve. *Jesus* means "Savior"; it was the name the angel told Joseph to give Mary's son "because he will save his people from their sins" (Matthew 1:21). *Christ* means "the *anointed* one"—the one promised in the Old Testament who came to serve as our Prophet, High Priest, and King.

Paul's greeting—"Grace and peace to you"—is really a prayer. He is asking that two of the priceless jewels of God's saving work might always remain with this congregation. Grace is the cause of our salvation. It is God's undeserved love that led him to provide a Savior from sin for us. Peace is the result of our salvation. It is the removal of any hostility between God and us, and it came about when Jesus paid for all our sins.

²We always thank God for all of you, mentioning you in our prayers. ³We continually remember before our God and Father your work produced by faith, your labor prompted by love, and your endurance inspired by hope in our Lord Jesus Christ.

Paul's letters usually begin with a prayer of thanksgiving. Here Paul declares that he gives thanks *every day* for *every one* of the Thessalonians! What a wonderful faith God had worked in the Thessalonian congregation—and can also work in ours today!

Three features stood out among the Thessalonians for which Paul gives thanks: their work, labor, and endurance. Note also the triad from which their work and labor and endurance flowed: faith, love, and hope. These God-given gifts produced the fruits in the Thessalonian lives for which Paul is so thankful.

By his Word, God had worked *faith* in these people's hearts. It was a faith that trusted God's promise that for Jesus' sake their sins were forgiven. This faith filled their hearts. It compelled them to find ways to thank God for his gracious gift of forgiveness. Deeds of obedience, kindness, and purity flowed from their faith. So Paul gives thanks for "your work produced by faith."

God's transforming love also worked *love* in these believers' hearts. This moved them to reach out to all in need, especially those in need of the Savior. The Thessalonians labored hard, no doubt with considerable investments of both time and money, to share the gospel of God's love with other people in Thessalonica. Later we'll see how they also labored to spread the gospel throughout the province of Macedonia and into the rest of the Roman Empire as well. This mission work flowed from their love. Thus Paul gives thanks for "your labor prompted by love."

Last but not least, the Lord filled their hearts with *hope,* making them certain that after this short life an eternity of joy awaited them in heaven. Such hope enabled them to remain faithful in spite of bitter persecution by the Jews. Their endurance in suffering flowed from the sure hope that was theirs in Christ. For this "hope in our Lord Jesus Christ" Paul also gives thanks.

All this Paul remembers in his prayer "before our God and Father." The world around us might never take note of our work produced by faith, our labor prompted by love, and our endurance inspired by hope. In fact, the world may despise all three. But our heavenly Father knows. And this is all that matters.

Because it might have seemed that no one noticed or cared, Paul assured the Thessalonians that God always takes note of his people's faithfulness. May this truth encourage and inspire us to be faithful like those early Christians!

God's Word works a firm faith

⁴For we know, brothers loved by God, that he has chosen you, ⁵because our gospel came to you not simply with words, but also with power, with the Holy Spirit and with deep conviction.

Faithfulness is a cause for rejoicing. At the same time it can be the cause of a dangerous sin—self-righteous pride. Christians need to beware lest they think their faithfulness is their own accomplishment. Paul has just spoken glowing words about the Thessalonians. Now he quickly reminds them who is really responsible for all they have accomplished. It is God. God has loved them and chosen them to be his faithful people, even before the world was made.

The word used for "love" here in the Greek is *agape*. It is a love that loves even when there is no reason to love. There was nothing about the Thessalonians that made them lovable to God, but in his grace God did so anyway. The tense of the verb in Greek indicates this was a loving that God had done in the past and that the result of this loving was still in effect.

When Paul adds "he has chosen you," we know exactly when in the past God had "loved" the Thessalonians. The choosing to which Paul refers is the love that God showed to all believers before the world was created. Already then God had chosen them to be his own dear children by faith in Jesus.

We usually refer to this choosing of believers from eternity as our *election*. It is described more fully by Paul in Ephesians 1:4-6,11-14 and in Romans 8:28-39, where he declares, "Those he predestined, he also called; those he called, he also justified. . . ."

Many people are mystified by the doctrine of election. It is beyond our understanding. But for a believer, especially in a time of trouble, it is a great comfort. This doctrine assures us that our salvation is not in our feeble hands but in God's almighty hands. God chose us from eternity, and in his grace he promises to keep us as his own to eternity. Although Paul refers to the doctrine of election only briefly in this letter, he knew the assurance that even this passing reference would give the Thessalonians in their trials. They were God's own from eternity to eternity. Nothing could ever snatch them from the Lord.

The effect the gospel produced in the Thessalonians was proof of their election. The gospel was not just so many words to the Thessalonians, but it also came to them "with power." It penetrated their stony hearts and turned them to faith in Jesus. The gospel was able to accomplish this because it came to them "with the Holy Spirit." The gospel was the means by which the Holy Spirit worked in their hearts with such power. And the gospel did not just affect the Thessalonians slightly, but it came to them "with deep conviction." They were willing to give up life, goods, fame, child, and wife rather than lose Christ.

Such were the astounding results that God's Word produced in the Thessalonians. And such—praise God!—are the results that God's Word works in the hearts of all of us whom he graciously chose to be his own before the creation of the world. Paul's words still resound to believers today: "We know . . . that he has chosen you."

The Thessalonians' faithfulness—a model for others

You know how we lived among you for your sake. ⁶You became imitators of us and of the Lord; in spite of severe suffering, you welcomed the message with the joy given by the Holy Spirit.

Previously Paul had reviewed the wonderful results the gospel had produced in the Thessalonians. Now he reminds them that they in turn knew how he, Silas, and Timothy had lived among them. Paul will expand on this later. He mentions it here only by way of introducing a second truth he knows about the Thessalonians. This truth is another reason why he is sure God has chosen them.

In spite of the fact that they were suffering persecution, they "welcomed the message with the joy given by the Holy Spirit." How could anyone be joyful in the middle of persecution? Numerous Scripture passages answer that question. For example, Romans 5:3,4 describes some blessed results from trials: "We also rejoice in our sufferings, because we know that suffering produces perseverance; perseverance, character; and character, hope."

By faith in Jesus we have forgiveness and peace with God. Therefore, we also know that God uses everything in our lives to bring us closer to himself so that we may be his forever. As a result we can rejoice even in our sufferings, because we know they too serve God's saving purpose in our lives.

Unbelievers cannot see how there can be joy in any kind of suffering, much less the "severe suffering" the Thessalonians were experiencing. But the "joy given by the Holy Spirit" assured the Thessalonians that their Savior was watching over them. This led them to be willing to suffer for Jesus' sake and to do so with joy. They followed the apostles who rejoiced "because they had been counted worthy of suffering for the Name" of Christ (Acts 5:41).

In this way the Thessalonians "became imitators" of Paul. In Philippi, the city Paul visited just before he came to Thessalonica, Paul's life had been threatened. Trouble also pursued him when he left Thessalonica and went on to the next city, Berea. Paul's pattern of clinging to God's Word and rejoicing in tribulation had become a model that the Thessalonians imitated.

They also "became imitators" of their Lord Jesus. Peter points out how Jesus serves as an example for all Christians to imitate in suffering: "Christ suffered for you, leaving you an example, that you should follow in his steps. When they hurled their insults at him, he did not retaliate; when he suffered, he made no threats. Instead, he entrusted himself to him who judges justly" (1 Peter 2:21,23).

Think how Paul's words must have encouraged the Thessalonians when his letter was read to them! Are you undergoing any kind of trial at this time? May Christ's saving love for you shine through that dark cloud. May you, like the Thessalonians, welcome his message with "the joy given by the Holy Spirit."

⁷And so you became a model to all the believers in Macedonia and Achaia. ⁸The Lord's message rang out from you not only in Macedonia and Achaia—your faith in God has become known everywhere.

The Thessalonians imitated Paul and Jesus in their suffering. In doing so they became a pattern for all the Christians in the surrounding regions. Nor did it stop there. Their faith served as a model throughout the entire Christian church.

When we remember that Thessalonica was one of the most important crossroad cities in the Roman Empire, it is easy to understand how word about the congregation in Thessalonica would spread rapidly both east and west. Visitors who passed through the city often stopped to rest a day or two. This would give Christian travelers an opportunity to make contact with the Christian congregation in the city. What they learned in that short visit made a deep impression on them.

They found Christians who were under constant threat of persecution, yet whose love for Christ and whose joy in the gospel were both obvious and inspiring. Many a traveler must have left Thessalonica saying to himself or herself, "They suffer so much for the name of Christ, and I so little. Their faith and love and hope are so alive. Lord, fill me with a faith like theirs!"

Paul describes the Thessalonian congregation as a bell whose ringing filled the ears of Christians in Macedonia and Achaia (the northern and southern halves of Greece) and the neighboring parts of the Roman Empire. The message their ringing proclaimed was loud and clear. It was the "Lord's message." It was the message that what he did for sinful men made a difference.

Christ's redeeming love gave the Thessalonians a reason to live—to share that love with others. Christ's love removed the sting of persecution, suffering, and death. They had the sure hope that they belonged to their Lord for time and eternity.

Are we Christians today bells that ring out the message of the Savior's love in our neighborhood, our country, our world? Are we models after whom visitors to our congregation want to pattern themselves? Would we like to be? Let's go on reading as Paul reveals more about the simple yet effective secret of the Thessalonians' faith.

Therefore we do not need to say anything about it, ⁹for they themselves report what kind of reception you gave us. They tell how you turned to God from idols to serve the living and true God, ¹⁰and to wait for his Son from heaven, whom he raised from the dead— Jesus, who rescues us from the coming wrath.

Paul quickly discovered that whenever he entered into a conversation with a Christian who had visited in Thessalonica, it wasn't necessary to say anything about the wonderful miracle God had accomplished there. Before Paul could even mention his experience in founding that congregation, the visitor would give Paul a complete report of everything that had happened.

First the visitor would tell Paul all about how the Thessalonians had received Paul. Imagine, instead of Paul telling his own story, these people told Paul the story about himself in Thessalonica! We can just see Paul standing there listening with a smile on his face as he heard each new person coming from Thessalonica telling him the old familiar story. He listened gladly because he didn't want to dampen the joy these people had experienced in their visit to Thessalonica and now had to share, even with the man who knew the full story better than they.

It must have warmed Paul's heart even more when the visitors went on to describe how the Thessalonians who once worshiped idols had turned to the living God. These people had once bowed down to gods made of wood, stone, gold, and silver—gods made with their own hands. Now they knew the true God. They knew that the true God was not made from created things but that he was the Creator of all things. They knew he was a God who was living and could and would fulfill all his threats and promises. He was a God who demanded his whole creation to be holy as he was holy. And they knew this living God was a God of love who sent his only Son to give his life for a sinful world that otherwise would have been lost forever.

The visitors reported it was obvious that the Thessalonians had "turned" to God. They had turned completely away from their idols. There were no regrets that they had left an old way of life for a completely new one. They had no second thoughts about the sinful pleasures they had left behind, no longing for the wealth or fame that some of them must have lost because of the persecution that was their lot as Christians in Thessalonica. Instead of regrets, they were filled with the desire "to serve the living and true God."

We saw earlier how they served God with their "work produced by faith, labor prompted by love, and . . . endurance inspired by hope." Paul's smile must have grown wider when he heard these visitors declare that they were going to make the Thessalonians a model for their own lives.

But Paul had still more reasons for rejoicing in these reports. They went on to relate that the Thessalonians were waiting eagerly for Jesus' return. As they busied themselves in service for their Lord, the Thessalonians always had one

15

eye looking heavenward. The thought was always with them: "Are you coming today, Lord?"

They knew exactly for whom they were waiting. They were waiting for God's own Son from heaven. They knew he was the same Jesus who had been born in Bethlehem and died on Calvary's cross. But God had raised him from the dead. This, they knew, was God's seal of approval on Jesus' atoning work. And so they confidently waited for his promised return.

They also knew exactly why they were waiting for him. Jesus was their "rescuer." The term *rescue* emphasizes both the peril of the person rescued and the power of the rescuer. The Thessalonians were aware of their helpless condition in face of "the coming wrath." They, like all mankind, would someday appear before the judgment throne of God to answer for their sins.

By faith these people were assured that Jesus had rescued them from the coming wrath of God. When he came to earth the first time, Jesus Christ had removed sin's guilt and condemnation. On the cross he took upon himself God's wrath for all people's sins. So whenever Jesus would come again, they could be sure he was coming to take them safely home to heaven. There forever they would rejoice in God's presence. For that day they eagerly waited.

Serving the living and true God and waiting for his Son from heaven is a short yet comprehensive description of what the Christian's life is all about. Remember, this was not the result of a faith that the Thessalonians worked in themselves. Rather, God's Word produced this faith in them.

The Thessalonians are a model for us. We can't work ourselves up to this model, but God can and does work it in those who make his Word the center of their lives.

May the gospel also come to us "not simply with words, but also with power, with the Holy Spirit and with deep conviction" (1:5). And may God in this way also turn us from all the idols of our day to serve him as we wait for his Son from heaven!

PART TWO

The Work of a Faithful Pastor
(2:1-12)

He is bold in the face of opposition

2 **You know, brothers, that our visit to you was not a failure. ²We had previously suffered and been insulted in Philippi, as you know, but with the help of our God we dared to tell you this gospel in spite of strong opposition.**

Paul now turns to a rather lengthy description of the faithful ministry he had carried on "with the help of God" in Thessalonica. Note how Paul gives God the credit for everything he accomplished as a pastor.

But why does the apostle spend 12 verses talking about himself? Surely not to beat his own drum. Two other reasons readily suggest themselves. One is to encourage the persecuted Thessalonians. If God had kept Paul faithful amid trials, he could do the same for them.

A second reason becomes obvious as we read these verses. Apparently there were some people, maybe the persecutors, who were suggesting that Paul's ministry was self-serving. There seems to have been implications that, like many unscrupulous traveling teachers of the day, Paul had come to Thessalonica only long enough to make a name for himself and to get whatever money he could out of the people—and then had hurried on to the next city.

It was true that Paul had spent only a few weeks among the Thessalonians, but he sets the record straight about his reasons for coming and about his love for them as a pastor.

He appeals to their awareness that his visit to them "was not a failure." Just prior to coming to Thessalonica, Paul and Silas had "suffered and been insulted in Philippi." (See Acts 16.) They were arrested, dragged before the authorities in the public marketplace, stripped of their clothes, and beaten with a whip that made deep cuts in their flesh. Then they were fastened by the feet in stocks and locked in a cell deep in the city prison. The insult of which Paul speaks was that in spite of their rights as Roman citizens, they had been beaten publicly without a trial.

After such experiences, who would have blamed Paul if he had quit preaching entirely or at least for a little while? This is especially true when in Thessalonica he ran into some immediate and bitter opposition again. But Paul did not quit. He did not even hold back a little bit. Instead, he appeals to the Thessalonians' memories of how he "dared" to tell them Christ's gospel in spite of the threat of bodily harm that stared him in the face so soon again after leaving Philippi.

Every faithful pastor needs this kind of boldness. God must still supply it. Without such courage a preacher undermines his own message. A pastor cannot shrink back from any threats of harm or ridicule that try to silence his proclaiming the good news about Christ our Savior. A faithful pastor is bold in the face of opposition so that he doesn't deny Christ.

He looks on his work as a sacred trust

[3]For the appeal we make does not spring from error or impure motives, nor are we trying to trick you. [4]On the contrary, we speak as men approved by God to be entrusted with the gospel. We are not trying to please men but God, who tests our hearts.

Many traveling teachers in the Roman Empire had reputations. Some claimed to be experts in what they taught, while in reality they themselves hadn't really mastered their subjects, such as math or science. Consequently, what they taught was full of errors. Some teachers had purely selfish motives for teaching. Instead of sharing their knowledge for the benefit of others, they were concerned only how they could benefit themselves. Some used oratory tricks or magical tricks done by sleight of hand or illusions that gave the appearance of strength or wisdom—all to hide their errors or to benefit themselves.

Paul flatly rejects any comparison between himself and such teachers. The apostle states that everything he taught was centered in the gospel and was spoken by him exactly the way God had directed.

Paul had not become an apostle by his own choosing. No, Christ had appeared to him on the road to Damascus and ended his self-chosen career as a persecutor of Christians. Jesus had called him to the unlikely position of a preacher of the gospel. Even then Paul had not struck out on his own to preach about Christ as he, Paul, might have thought best. Instead, for several years the Lord himself taught Paul the gospel that he was to preach to others. "I want you to know, brothers," Paul wrote to the Galatians, "that the gospel I preached is not something that man made up. But when God . . . was pleased to reveal his Son to me so that I might preach him among the Gentiles, I did not consult with any man" (1:11,15,16).

Paul took this matter seriously. He never departed from what God entrusted to him just to say something pleasing to his listeners. Thus he never became entangled in errors, impure motives, or attempts to trick people. Rather, he spoke only that which pleased God, who "tests our hearts." Paul knew that receiving a trust from God required faithfulness. In God's court even the motives of one's heart will be examined in regard to one's faithfulness. In 1 Corinthians 4:1-4,

Paul expresses these truths: "So then, men ought to regard us as servants of Christ and as those entrusted with the secret things of God. Now it is required that those who have been given a trust must prove faithful. I care very little if I am judged by you or by any human court; indeed, I do not even judge myself. My conscience is clear, but that does not make me innocent. It is the Lord who judges me."

A second characteristic of a faithful pastor, then, is that he looks on his work as a sacred trust. It is not a work that he carries out in a way that pleases men but in a way that is God-pleasing—a way in which even the motives hidden in his heart will be found by God to be genuine.

He is as unselfish as a gentle mother

5You know we never used flattery, nor did we put on a mask to cover up greed—God is our witness. 6We were not looking for praise from men, not from you or anyone else.

As apostles of Christ we could have been a burden to you, 7but we were gentle among you, like a mother caring for her little children.

If you had a mother who was always ready to serve your happiness, often at the expense of what she might have wanted for herself, you can't help speaking of her in terms of glowing praise. Such was the unselfish kind of pastor Paul sought to be in his service to the Thessalonians.

We all know what flattery is: insincere praise. Usually it flows from selfishness, because the one who flatters is not speaking for the other person's good but is trying to manipulate him. Since Paul was concerned for the Thessalonians' souls, flattery was something he completely disavowed.

Moreover, his concern for their souls removed any selfishness in the form of greed. Perhaps some of the Thessalonians did have more money and comforts than Paul did, but Paul wasn't envious. Since they could not look into his heart

21

to examine the truth of this claim, Paul calls on God as his witness that he never masked any feelings of greed.

Paul often received praise from the people to whom he preached the gospel. But, the apostle declares, he didn't go looking for such praise—from the Thessalonians or anyone else. He did not do his mission work just so people would praise him.

Since Paul was an apostle, and since Silas and Timothy were his companions on this mission journey, they would have had every right to expect the Thessalonians to supply them with basic needs such as housing, food, and clothing. In 1 Corinthians 9:1-14 Paul spells out in detail the right of a teacher of God's Word to expect support from those who are taught. But as a matter of principle, Paul himself usually refused to take any support from the new congregations he founded. He did not want to give anyone the opportunity to accuse him of doing this work for the money. One notable exception to this rule was the Philippian congregation.

Instead of being a "burden" to them, Paul describes himself as a gentle nursing mother. It would be absurd for a mother to demand that her little baby support her. No, a mother who is loving and kind will do exactly the opposite. She will do everything her child's care demands: feeding, changing clothes, protecting, and helping the child in its every need. Perhaps the most vivid example of a mother's care is when she holds a baby gently in her arms and nourishes it at her breast. Paul wants the Thessalonians to recall him as having been such a "mother" to them.

Here is another picture of the ideal Christian pastor. He unselfishly cares for the people in his congregation without any thought of what he can get out of them. He does not manipulate people with flattery nor envy those members who live better than he nor does he work just for the praise it brings him. Instead he is one whose unselfishness is very similar to that of a gentle mother nursing her beloved child at her breast.

He is an untiring worker

⁸We loved you so much that we were delighted to share with you not only the gospel of God but our lives as well, because you had become so dear to us. ⁹Surely you remember, brothers, our toil and hardship; we worked night and day in order not to be a burden to anyone while we preached the gospel of God to you.

Twice within one verse Paul unashamedly expresses his deep love for the Thessalonians. These were not just words; they were words based on deeds. Paul's ministry was never just a "nine-to-five" job to him. He threw his whole heart and life into it. He loved the Thessalonians so dearly that he couldn't stop with just sharing the gospel with them. He had to share his life as well.

Paul points to his untiring work for their benefit as proof of his love. By day he would preach the gospel to any and all who would listen. He would instruct, comfort, and encourage individuals or small groups day by day. Then, late into the night he would work with his hands at a trade to make enough money to supply his and his companions' basic needs. Most likely he worked at tentmaking, which was a trade he had learned as a boy. Thus Paul's life was a "toil and hardship." That is, it was a life of hard work over long hours under some very trying circumstances.

Every pastor's love for his people will be evident in the work he does for them. Does a depressed individual need encouragement early in the morning? Does a small group need the information class to be conducted at a special time to meet their schedule? Does a call come just before supper for an emergency baptism or at midnight for a person who needs strengthening in the last hour of her life? Does a teenager or an engaged couple need counseling? By his unselfish life of service, the faithful pastor answers, "I love you so much that I am delighted to share with you, not only the gospel but my life as well, because you have become so dear to me."

He is like a father caring for his children

[10]**You are witnesses, and so is God, of how holy, righteous and blameless we were among you who believed.** [11]**For you know that we dealt with each of you as a father deals with his own children,** [12]**encouraging, comforting and urging you to live lives worthy of God, who calls you into his kingdom and glory.**

A teacher in a classroom can easily fall into the mistake of treating a class of 25 students as one mass instead of as 25 individuals. But a father who really cares about his children will never treat them all the same. He will train each one according to his or her unique abilities and personality.

Just as Paul had compared his care for the people to that of a loving mother, he now likens himself and his coworkers to a father. Part of a father's work of training each child is to set a pattern for his children to follow. This Paul sought to do when he as a "father" dealt with "each" of the Thessalonians. The words "holy, righteous, and blameless" all say the same thing about Paul's conduct, and yet each says it with a slightly different emphasis. *Holy* refers to the standard that God gives us in his law as a guide for what is right. *Righteous* refers to the approval God gives, in this instance the declaration that Paul's dealing with each of the Thessalonians was acceptable to God. *Blameless* refers to the inability of anyone to bring a charge against Paul's conduct.

Does Paul mean by this claim, which he calls on both the Thessalonians and God to witness, that he lived a perfect life without any sin while he was in Thessalonica? Not at all, as Paul makes clear in other passages such as Romans chapter 7, where he speaks of his sad failures in Christian living because of his sinful nature. Paul is only emphasizing that in his training them as a father he had followed a pattern set by God himself. This is *how* Paul dealt with them as his children. *What* he did follows.

The three verbs Paul uses to describe what he did as a father are again very similar to one another in thought but slightly different in emphasis. Remember that this letter is being written to people who were suffering a persecution that had begun already when Paul was in Thessalonica. Then each of these three terms will take on a very concrete meaning. The Thessalonians needed encouragement in their severe sufferings and trials. They needed comfort when in their trying situation they suffered the added loss of a loved one by death. A special, uplifting, cheering word was needed by each of them to continue living as God's dear children. In persecution they might be tempted to turn away from such a God-pleasing life, because of the trouble it brought them. Paul urged them to keep in mind the glorious eternal home awaiting them beyond this brief but difficult pilgrimage.

The final characteristic of the faithful pastor, then, is the way he cares for each soul entrusted to him in the same way as a father watches over each one of his children. He counsels and encourages each member according to his personal spiritual situation.

What a marvelous pastor Paul must have been! But he was the first to declare that the glory must all be God's. Only by the Almighty's strength was Paul able to serve so faithfully in the ministry. May God bless all our churches with such pastors who by God's help carry out their work boldly, faithfully, unselfishly, untiringly, and in a fatherly manner!

PART THREE

Faithful Endurance in Persecution
(2:13–3:9)

God's Word works faithfulness in persecution

¹³And we also thank God continually because, when you received the word of God, which you heard from us, you accepted it not as the word of men, but as it actually is, the word of God, which is at work in you who believe. ¹⁴For you, brothers, became imitators of God's churches in Judea, which are in Christ Jesus: You suffered from your own countrymen the same things those churches suffered from the Jews, ¹⁵who killed the Lord Jesus and the prophets and also drove us out.

Paul had opened this letter with a prayer of thanksgiving for the faithfulness that God's Word had worked in the Thessalonians. Now he repeats that prayer. This time he emphasizes the main thing that had prompted this letter—their faithfulness in the face of a terrible persecution.

When Paul first brought the Word of God to the Thessalonians, Paul had not changed or added anything to it. He preached it exactly as God gave it to him. None of it could be labeled as human opinion or a human philosophy. Rather, what the Thessalonians received was what it truly was—God's own message to them.

Paul emphasizes that if it had been man's word in any way, it could never have produced the marvelous faithfulness that it did. But because it was God's Word, it worked effectively and continually to sustain their faith in spite of their constant suffering at the hands of persecutors.

God's Word is a "power" (Romans 1:16) that is "living and active" (Hebrews 4:12) and so works a "deep conviction" (1 Thessalonians 1:5) in a believer's heart. But if God's pure Word is adulterated with human error, then the purity of God's Word is lost, and its effectiveness is greatly lessened or even completely destroyed.

As proof of the effective working of God's Word, Paul points to the Thessalonians' continued faith in spite of the fierce opposition by the Jews in Thessalonica.

The suffering of Christians at the hands of Jews was not anything new. It was the same right from the start of the Christian church in Jerusalem and in the surrounding cities and towns of Judea. The Jews had opposed God's prophets in the Old Testament. They had rejected and killed the Messiah himself. Following Christ's ascension, their opposition continued in the same bitter fashion against Christ's followers. It started with threatening and then arresting the apostles (Acts 4). Next they flogged the apostles (Acts 5) and put one of the deacons, Stephen, to death (Acts 7). Then came a full-scale persecution, including arrest, imprisonment, and death for many Christian laypeople (Acts 8). When the leader of the persecution, Saul, was converted to Christianity, they refused to listen to him and plotted his death too (Acts 9).

In Thessalonica history was repeating itself. The Thessalonians were suffering exactly the same persecutions from the Jews as the Christians in Judea had suffered. But Paul thanked God that there was another similarity between the Christians in Judea and in Thessalonica: God's Word was at work in them to preserve them in their faith.

The Jews opposed God's Word to their own condemnation

They displease God and are hostile to all men [16]**in their effort to keep us from speaking to the Gentiles so that they may be saved.**

27

In this way they always heap up their sins to the limit. The wrath of God has come upon them at last.

The Thessalonians might have expected persecution at the hands of the pagan Gentiles, but it must have come as a surprise to them to be persecuted by those who were God's chosen people in the Old Testament. Paul explains the Jewish opposition to the gospel in a few words.

"They displease God," Paul begins. What an understatement! As Stephen reminded the leaders of the Jews before they stoned him to death, the history of the Jews was filled with one rebellion against God after another in spite of the love and mercy that God showered on them.

In persecuting the Thessalonians and other Gentiles, another chapter of their displeasing rebellion was being written. Ordinarily the Jews would not have cared what the Gentiles did or believed. If the Jews had opposed only the conversion of Jews to Christianity, there would have been at least a little rhyme and reason to their opposition. But for them to try to prevent the conversion of Gentiles shows how bitter and unreasoning their actions were. The only explanation for such hostility toward the gospel, even when it was preached to Gentiles whom the Jews despised, was their characteristic rebellion against God's will.

"In this way," Paul says, they are doing what they "always" do—they keep the cup of their sins full to the brim. They had filled that cup by opposing the prophets and killing Christ. Now in their unbelief they insist on keeping it full by their senseless persecution of Gentiles.

With no joy, Paul adds the comment that God's anger with their continual rebellion had finally reached the stage in which God hardened them in their sin. In Romans 11:7 Paul writes that the Old Testament prophecy was fulfilled in which God says his patience with the Jews would end and he would give them "a spirit of stupor, eyes so that they could not see and ears so that they could not hear."

Such will always be the result of a persistent refusal on the part of any person to listen to God's Word when it is continually preached to him. Finally God's patience will end and God will harden him in his unbelief. The sad example of the Jews is a warning for us too not to despise the means of grace, lest God take them from us. "Do not be deceived: God cannot be mocked" (Galatians 6:7).

Paul sent Timothy to strengthen the Thessalonians

¹⁷**But, brothers, when we were torn away from you for a short time (in person, not in thought), out of our intense longing we made every effort to see you. ¹⁸For we wanted to come to you— certainly I, Paul, did, again and again—but Satan stopped us. ¹⁹For what is our hope, our joy, or the crown in which we will glory in the presence of our Lord Jesus when he comes? Is it not you? ²⁰Indeed, you are our glory and joy.**

3 So when we could stand it no longer, we thought it best to be left by ourselves in Athens. ²We sent Timothy, who is our brother and God's fellow worker in spreading the gospel of Christ, to strengthen and encourage you in your faith, ³so that no one would be unsettled by these trials.

At this point in the letter, Paul opens his heart and lets the Thessalonians see the emotions that were raging there since the time that he had left Thessalonica.

Angered by the success of Paul's preaching in Thessalonica, the Jews had instigated a riot, and Paul had been forced to flee the city under cover of darkness. He refers to this when he states "we were torn away" with no chance to say any words of farewell. Ever since then his thoughts kept turning back to them. He had made a number of plans to return to Thessalonica because he longed to see them again and strengthen them. But Satan prevented every such attempt.

Apparently Paul had hoped that the Jews' opposition to gospel preaching in Thessalonica might cool down so he could return. It just didn't happen. This red-hot fire of opposition that Satan kept fanning not only kept Paul from coming back, but its continuing intensity made Paul worry all the more about whether the Thessalonians were holding fast to the faith.

During these anxious days, Paul looked ahead to the Last Day when all believers would be gathered in Christ's presence to live with him forever. What if the Thessalonians would fall from faith and wouldn't be there? He loved the Thessalonians so dearly, his hope was so vitally connected with theirs, that without them it would be somewhat hollow. His joy was so entwined with theirs that without them it would not seem full. When Paul stood before Christ's throne, he wanted to do so with all those whom God brought to faith by his preaching. They would be his crown. They would be the proof of God's blessing on his work as a gospel preacher.

As Paul thought about the possibility that his beloved in Thessalonica might despair and turn from Christ, and as the days turned into weeks and the weeks into months, and when finally he couldn't stand the waiting and wondering any longer—he sent Timothy to them. If Paul himself could not return, then his right-hand man would go. Timothy had not been with Paul very long, and he was young, but he had already proven himself a true brother in the faith and an able teacher of the gospel. Timothy would go and firm up those Thessalonians whom the persecution was beginning to unsettle and weaken.

It was not easy for Paul to part with Timothy even for a short while. Paul was in Athens, a city filled with idols and, at the same time, a university town very skeptical of any religion that taught such "nonsense" as the resurrection of the dead.

Paul needed Timothy badly, both as a "fellow worker" for support in his preaching and as a "brother" in maintaining his own faith amid a situation so hostile to Christian faith. Nevertheless, the troubles in Thessalonica weighed so heavily on Paul that he determined to go it alone in Athens. The Greek word literally means to be "orphaned" or "abandoned" in Athens. No matter. The Thessalonians must be helped. His own personal need for Timothy must take second place.

Paul feared for their faith

You know quite well that we were destined for them. ⁴In fact, when we were with you, we kept telling you that we would be persecuted. And it turned out that way, as you well know. ⁵For this reason, when I could stand it no longer, I sent to find out about your faith. I was afraid that in some way the tempter might have tempted you and our efforts might have been useless.

Christians will be persecuted for their faith. Jesus tells all his followers that the hatred aimed at him while he was on earth would continue against his disciples after he ascended. "If they persecuted me, they will persecute you also" (John 15:20). Paul told the Christians on his first mission journey, "We must go through many hardships to enter the kingdom of God" (Acts 14:22). Paul had also warned the Thessalonians that as Christians they were destined for trials.

Indeed, he had given them a special forewarning of the persecution for which they were destined. More than once during those few short weeks when he was with them he had spoken about this. And then came the day when a mob rioted against Paul's preaching and triggered a persecution that had continued unabated ever since.

Yet even Paul must have been surprised by the ferocity of the persecution and its length. As he had mentioned earlier, his fears finally got the best of him, and he just had to know something about the situation.

Why was Paul afraid of what might have happened? Simply because he knew Satan was behind the persecution. The devil's power is a mighty force against a Christian's faith. The struggle against Satan is very difficult because it is not a struggle "against flesh and blood, but against . . . the powers of this dark world and against the spiritual forces of evil in the heavenly realms" (Ephesians 6:12). Eve succumbed to Satan's tempting. So did Judas. So also could the Thessalonians if someone did not strengthen them with "the full armor of God" (Ephesians 6:13). This Paul sent Timothy to do.

While Timothy was gone, Paul finished his work in Athens and moved on to Corinth to begin a new mission thrust. All the while he anxiously awaited Timothy's return.

Timothy's report gave Paul great joy

⁶But Timothy has just now come to us from you and has brought good news about your faith and love. He has told us that you always have pleasant memories of us and that you long to see us, just as we also long to see you. ⁷Therefore, brothers, in all our distress and persecution we were encouraged about you because of your faith. ⁸For now we really live, since you are standing firm in the Lord. ⁹How can we thank God enough for you in return for all the joy we have in the presence of our God because of you?

Finally Timothy returned. He brought the good news that the Thessalonians had remained faithful in the persecution. He also reassured Paul of their continued love and concern for him, the man who had first brought them the good news of Christ their Savior. They hadn't turned against Paul, even though their sufferings were a direct result of his preaching. Quite to the contrary, they recalled those weeks of Paul's visit with fond memories. Paul had risked his life to share the message of eternal joy with them. They could never forget that. They wanted to see Paul as much as he wanted to see them again.

Timothy's report uplifted Paul. It seems that Paul's ministry in Athens had gained only a few souls for Christ. This, together with the successive persecutions in Philippi, Thessalonica, and Berea, was almost too much for the apostle.

When Paul arrived in Corinth, he once again began to experience the same persecution from the Jews. In a vision the Lord encouraged Paul to preach and renewed his promise of protection. The news from Thessalonica was another tremendous encouragement to Paul. Paul was a man of deep emotions, and he had been, as it were, dying a slow death in his anxiety over his beloved and persecuted Thessalonians.

Now Paul knew they were standing firm, not retreating an inch in the face of Satan's onslaughts by the Jews. He could really live again. He could take up the preaching of the gospel with renewed vigor.

Paul was so excited and happy with Timothy's report that words actually failed him when he tried to express his thanks to God for what God had done in Thessalonica. God had not only kept the Thessalonians faithful but had made them a bell that rang the message about Christ through all of Macedonia and Greece. No earthly joy could compare with the joy that filled Paul's heart "in the presence of God" because of them. Here Paul, the great master of words, could only ask, "How can we thank God enough?"

As we close this section, two things stand out. One is Satan's bitter attack upon all gospel preaching. He can get people to do his dirty work, even though it doesn't make any real sense for them to be opposed to the gospel. The other is the awesome power of God's Holy Spirit to keep Christians in the faith in spite of everything Satan throws their way.

The devil hasn't changed. In our day and in our land, he continues to oppose the gospel. It may not be in the form of a persecution that threatens the loss of our possessions, imprisonment, or death. It might simply come as ridicule. Perhaps we are considered unintellectual or socially backward. Satan uses whatever roadblocks he can throw in our way by whatever people he can sway to serve him. We need to be constant in our use of the means of grace and in prayers for one another.

In other countries our fellow Christians may have to suffer more for the gospel than we do. Like Paul, let us express our oneness with them by sending pastors and teachers to strengthen them and by earnestly praying for them. We will be uplifted as they stand firm.

PART FOUR

Living to Please God
(3:10–4:12)

Paul prays that God may increase their faith and love

[10]Night and day we pray most earnestly that we may see you again and supply what is lacking in your faith.

[11]Now may our God and Father himself and our Lord Jesus clear the way for us to come to you. [12]May the Lord make your love increase and overflow for each other and for everyone else, just as ours does for you. [13]May he strengthen your hearts so that you will be blameless and holy in the presence of our God and Father when our Lord Jesus comes with all his holy ones.

The fact that Timothy's report was such a good one did not mean Paul would forget about the Thessalonians. He kept praying that he would be able to visit them soon. The persecution still went on. The Thessalonians needed to be strengthened in their faith and devotion to Christ. Whatever they lacked in their faith Paul wanted to supply by seeing them and sharing God's Word with them again.

But unless Satan's roadblocks were removed, Paul knew he would never get back to Thessalonica. He realized that the only one who could clear the way was God himself. So Paul prayed that God would put enough of a damper on the persecution so he could return without foolishly endangering his own life and without stirring up even greater suffering for the believers in Thessalonica.

Lest the Thessalonians feel they could not grow in faith without a visit from Paul, he adds a third prayer. In this prayer he asks the Lord to bless and strengthen the Thessalonians. He reminds them it is really God, not Paul, who sustains them.

Paul asks that the Lord would increase their love to the point of overflowing. Like a cup that fills with water and then overflows, so Paul prays that their hearts might overflow with love. As on a hot day we fill a cup with cold water, letting the delightful sparkling liquid splash over into our hands, so a Christian's love brings joy to all it touches.

God had brought these people into a new spiritual family by faith: a family in which each member was responsible for the other. All worked together for the good of the whole family. Here was a family in which strengthening, comforting, and encouragement of one another from God's Word was a daily experience—especially in their present persecution. So they were to love one another.

Nor does Christian love stop within the family of believers. It overflows for everyone else as well: love for unbelieving neighbors and friends, expressed in deeds as well as words; love for government officials and employers, expressed in Christian subordination; and, yes, love also for the Jews who were persecuting Christians, just as Christ loved his enemies and prayed for them.

Paul can't refrain from adding a reminder of his own love for them. He urges that their love overflow "just as ours does for you." With these words he encourages the Thessalonians to be imitators of himself, Silas, and Timothy, in love just as they had followed them in enduring persecution.

Paul adds the result of making their love increase to overflowing. They would be "blameless and holy" when Christ comes on the Last Day. The "strengthen[ing of] your hearts" of which Paul speaks is an inner strength—their whole inner beings, their thoughts and their feelings. God looks past the outward actions people perform. He searches the heart to see whether their actions are born of faith in Christ, actions done to thank Christ for his saving work. Any action, no matter how beneficial to others, is not pleasing to God unless it flows from a heart filled with such faith. As Hebrews 11:6 states, "Without faith it is impossible to please God." Deeds of love that flow from faith are proof that faith is alive and well.

Someday, when Jesus returns in glory, everyone will stand "in the presence" of God and be judged. Believers will be known by the deeds of faith that Christ recounts: "Another book was opened, which is the book of life. The dead were judged according to what they had done as recorded in the books" (Revelation 20:12).

It is often debated whether Jesus' coming "with all his holy ones" means with the angels or with believers. The expression "holy ones" is an expression that Paul uses elsewhere in his letters only to refer to believers. Here Paul has just finished speaking of believers being blameless in holiness. When Paul speaks of Christ coming "with all his holy ones," this simply refers to all those believers who have died and whose souls are with Christ in paradise. Later, in 4:15, Paul will speak of how these believers will return with Christ and share a glorious reunion with the living believers.

Paul's prayer for the Thessalonians is a beautiful prayer for us to use. Let us pray for our fellow believers, that our love for one another and everyone else might increase to overflowing. Then, when Christ comes in judgment, our deeds of love will stand as undeniable evidence of our living in Christ.

Paul urges them to live by his instructions

4 **Finally, brothers, we instructed you how to live in order to please God, as in fact you are living. Now we ask you and urge you in the Lord Jesus to do this more and more. ²For you know what instructions we gave you by the authority of the Lord Jesus.**

Paul has just prayed that the Thessalonians might over-flow in deeds of love. From this point on, his letter concerns itself with how God wants Christians to live.

Paul reminds his readers that when he was with them, he had given them some thorough instructions on this subject, even though he had been there only a very short time.

They had taken this instruction to heart and had begun patterning their lives according to what Paul had taught them was pleasing to God.

But they still had plenty of room for growth in Christian living. To help them in that direction would be Paul's goal in the rest of this letter. Paul knew they would gladly receive everything he told them in this regard, so he does not admonish or threaten them. Rather, he asks and urges.

He does this asking and urging "in the Lord Jesus." Paul did not want their motive for Christian living to be one of pleasing Paul. No, he wanted their Christian lives to be motivated and empowered by Christ. Christ, not Paul, had lived and died for them. Christ, not Paul, had set them free from sin and death and made them heirs of eternal life. Paul's words to the Colossians (3:17) applied to the Thessalonians (and apply to us today): "Whatever you do, whether in word or deed, do it all in the name of the Lord Jesus, giving thanks to God the Father through him."

Why does Paul add the remark that they knew all of the instructions he gave them were "by the authority of the Lord Jesus" himself? Verse 8 gives a hint. There Paul stresses that to reject his instruction was not just a rejection of man but of God.

In our struggle with our sinful nature, our old Adam, we need this reminder. The old Adam takes such pleasure in sin that it tries to convince us that living in the way it wants us to live really isn't so bad. It tries to persuade us that how we live is an individual matter, and we shouldn't let other people impose their standard of morality on us. It is then that we need Paul's reminder. The instructions about holy living found in the Bible are not man's but are given by the Lord Jesus.

God's will for sex and marriage

³It is God's will that you should be sanctified: that you should avoid sexual immorality; ⁴that each of you should learn to control his own body in a way that is holy and honorable, ⁵not in passionate lust like the heathen, who do not know God; ⁶and that in this matter no one should wrong his brother or take advantage of him. The Lord will punish men for all such sins, as we have already told you and warned you. ⁷For God did not call us to be impure, but to live a holy life. ⁸Therefore, he who rejects this instruction does not reject man but God, who gives you his Holy Spirit.

Sexual immorality was rampant at the time the New Testament was written. The Thessalonians lived in a society in which premarital sex and marital unfaithfulness were commonplace and considered normal. Paul reminds them, however, that God wants them to live lives quite different from those of their fellow men—lives in which they consciously and continually drown the sinful old Adam and put on the new man in the matter of sex and marriage.

God wants his people to "avoid sexual immorality." More literally these words could be translated "hold yourself completely apart from sinful sexual intercourse." Since our old Adam is quick to try to get us involved in sinful sex, we need to keep our distance from every situation in which the old Adam would have a chance to mislead us.

Paul applies this especially to our thoughts and actions in courtship leading to marriage. You will find various translations for verse 4 because the Greek word for "vessel" (KJV) or "body," footnote: "wife" (NIV), is a very general term. Perhaps the best translation in the context is, "Let each of you know how to obtain a marriage partner in a way that is holy and honorable."

Greek men often sought a wife as a sex object, or, as Paul puts it, "in passionate lust." They were most interested in how good looking a woman was. The more physically attractive a woman was, the more passionately they lusted to have sex with her.

This sounds familiar, doesn't it? Many popular love songs and love stories in movies and on TV today promote the same ideas in the matter of sex and marriage. You marry someone to have sex. If you can't wait, you have sex before you are married. Or, you have an affair while married or with someone who is married, simply because you are "in love" with that person.

God says all this is sin. It is a kind of sexual immorality from which Paul urges us to keep away. Instead the Lord wants us to go about finding and choosing our marriage partner "in a way that is holy and honorable." And remember, behind God's will lies his wisdom and his love. He gave marriage and the fulfillment of the sex drive as a gift of his love for us. He knows how we will be able to enjoy this gift to the fullest. The path God commands is the only one to follow, so that Satan will not be able to turn this gift to ashes in our mouths. The devil does this in the lives of many who follow the sinful passionate lusts that he promotes in their hearts.

As God's children, let us choose our marriage partners in the knowledge that marriage is a holy estate. It is an estate in which God joins a husband and wife together in a lifelong union. In this union God blesses us with companionship, sexual happiness, and children. If we keep this in mind, then the way we go about obtaining a marriage partner is bound to be different from the world around us. Paul says the people of the world "do not know God," so their ways should not surprise us. We, however, do know God. We need his wisdom and power to resist our sinful nature. With the Lord's help, we will strive to follow his way, rather than the way of the world that can influence us so easily.

Sex is part of marriage, so sexual attraction is an important part of choosing a marriage partner. But the "holy and honorable" way does not concentrate on whether he or she is sexy. It looks for a lifelong companion with whom one can share joys and sorrows, with whom one can share sex as an expression of oneness, and with whom one eagerly desires the gift of children to train for this life and the next. Perhaps Peter expressed the thought most simply when he described a Christian couple as those who live together "as heirs" with one another "of the gracious gift of life" (1 Peter 3:7).

Paul continues, "In this matter no one should wrong his brother or take advantage of him." Since the "matter" Paul has just spoken about is the choosing of a marriage partner, these words warn against any tampering with a relationship between a couple that is becoming very serious and obviously approaching engagement. If I "take advantage" of someone in such a relationship by using my looks or wealth to take the man or woman away from that person, I am doing wrong. Knowing what a precious gift of God marriage is, and knowing from these words of Paul that God wants us to be "holy and honorable" in choosing a marriage partner, how could I begin to toy around with courtship in such a way?

No sin in regard to marriage and sex should ever be a light matter to us: "The Lord will punish men for all such sins." All who engage in sexual immorality are calling down God's wrath upon themselves. Paul doesn't mention this to the Thessalonians merely in passing but gives them a crystal-clear warning because of the predominance of this sin in their society.

He repeats the warning later in this letter so it won't be forgotten. When the Lord calls a Christian to faith, he does not call that person "to be impure, but to live a holy life." God doesn't wash away our sins that we might return like "a dog returns to its vomit" or like "a sow that is washed goes back to her wallowing in the mud" (2 Peter 2:22).

Christ redeemed us from sin to make us his own. We are, in Luther's words, to "live under him in his kingdom, and serve him in everlasting righteousness, innocence, and blessedness." This means that we thank Christ by the holy lives we live also in the matter of sex and marriage.

Lest the Thessalonians forget, Paul again emphasizes that he is not imposing his own or some other man-made morality on them. This is God's holy will. To toss it aside as being out-of-date or hopelessly naive is a rejection of God himself, especially God the Holy Spirit.

Sexual sins are committed against that very body in which the Holy Spirit lives as his holy temple. The Spirit's dwelling in us, therefore, is totally incompatible with indulging ourselves in sexual immorality. "Flee from sexual immorality," Paul wrote elsewhere, ". . . You are not your own; you were bought at a price. Therefore honor God with your body" (1 Corinthians 6:18-20).

Being led by brotherly love

⁹Now about brotherly love we do not need to write to you, for you yourselves have been taught by God to love each other. ¹⁰And in fact, you do love all the brothers throughout Macedonia. Yet we urge you, brothers, to do so more and more.

¹¹Make it your ambition to lead a quiet life, to mind your own business and to work with your hands, just as we told you, ¹²so that

your daily life may win the respect of outsiders and so that you will not be dependent on anybody.

Paul moves on to another aspect of Christian living. It was rather common for Greek men to leave the manual labor to their wives and slaves. This left the men to spend their days in the marketplace. There they would gather to discuss political and economic issues, and (all too often) to indulge in idle gossip. Thus they often became busybodies in other people's affairs.

Paul urges the Thessalonians to gauge their lives in this matter not according to the way most people lived but according to the brotherly love God taught them. When did God teach them this subject? When he brought them to faith. As a person comes to believe in Jesus, his heart is filled with love for God. And hand in hand with love for God comes love for one's neighbor.

Saint John wrote that it is impossible for a person who loves God not to love his brother also: "We love because he first loved us. If anyone says, 'I love God,' yet hates his brother, he is a liar. For anyone who does not love his brother, whom he has seen, cannot love God, whom he has not seen. And he has given us this command: Whoever loves God must also love his brother" (1 John 4:19-21). These thoughts parallel Paul's.

Since the Thessalonians understood these truths, Paul says, "We do not need to write to you." This was all the more evident from the fact that the Thessalonians' love moved them to share the gospel throughout Macedonia.

But, as he has done before in this letter, Paul urges them to grow even more in their practice of brotherly love, especially in avoiding the idleness and gossiping of their neighbors.

The Greeks loved oratory. Greek men often had the ambition of using public speeches to sway large crowds. Oratory was one of the main studies Greek boys had to pursue. As well as producing great orators, this also resulted in a lot of loudmouths. In contrast to this, Paul urges the Christians to make it their "ambition to lead a quiet life." This didn't mean they should stop telling others about the gospel. Nevertheless, they were to limit their talk to what was wholesome and helpful, instead of pushy and overbearing.

Rather than avoiding manual labor and indulging in gossip, God wanted the brotherly love that he had taught them to lead them "to mind [their] own business and to work with [their] own hands." Paul wasn't saying they should never concern themselves with helping their neighbors or that it was wrong to make a living with one's head rather than with his hands. No, the point is the principle of brotherly love. Being a busybody while refusing to work and support oneself violated this principle. These unbrotherly, and thus sinful, actions are the object of Paul's admonition.

He gives two reasons for the admonition. The first is that if a Christian lives according to God's teaching about brotherly love, very often it will "win the respect of outsiders." Acts of brotherly love will touch a responsive chord in all but the most hardened, even outside the Christian church. These people also have God-given consciences and will respect what they know is right. Their respect for Christians' brotherly love might even be a tool God uses to prepare their hearts for the gospel.

Second, it is important that Christians don't become leeches who live off others. God wants his people to provide for their own needs so they are not "dependent on anybody." A person who refuses to work when work is available makes himself a nuisance.

Paul will have much more to say about idleness in his second letter. Apparently some members of the congregation continued in this sin despite Paul's admonition. We take up the whole matter of welfare and charity in more detail in our comments on 2 Thessalonians.

But isn't it interesting to see in this section, as Paul begins to discuss a life pleasing to God, how specific he becomes in his instruction? He speaks directly to the Thessalonians' problems. And did it strike you how Paul's words are just as pertinent for our lives today as they were for the Thessalonians? May we also take these instructions on sex and on brotherly love to heart! They are God's will for us. They teach us the way of true freedom and lasting happiness. May the Holy Spirit help us follow them in thanks to Christ for his goodness to us!

PART FIVE

The Coming of the Lord
(4:13–5:11)

Believers who have died will not be left behind when Christ comes

¹³**Brothers, we do not want you to be ignorant about those who fall asleep, or to grieve like the rest of men, who have no hope. ¹⁴We believe that Jesus died and rose again and so we believe that God will bring with Jesus those who have fallen asleep in him. ¹⁵According to the Lord's own word, we tell you that we who are still alive, who are left till the coming of the Lord, will certainly not precede those who have fallen asleep.**

Although the Thessalonians had been firm in the face of persecution, one thing bothered them. What about their fellow believers who died before Jesus returned in glory? Would they be lost because of this?

It seems in his short stay at Thessalonica, Paul hadn't had the opportunity to speak about this. He now knew their lack of knowledge about this point was disturbing them. They were concerned about their believing friends and loved ones who had passed away.

Before we look at what Paul said about this, note how he refers to these departed believers: *dead in Christ* and those who *sleep*. The use of the picture of sleep is no euphemism. Paul isn't just trying to make something bad seem a little bit better by referring to it in rosy terms. No, he is describing what death really is like for one who is dead in Christ. It is like a sleep in which a person's body is completely unaware of anything around it, but from which his body awakes to use all its abilities and senses again.

We aren't afraid to put our heads down on our pillows at night and go to sleep. We know we'll wake up again to a new day. That's how death is. We need not fear putting our heads down on the pillows of death and falling asleep. Jesus will wake us up to a glorious eternal day.

People without this sure hope will grieve in a way that shows they have no comfort. At best they might cling to some fond memories of their departed loved one. Or comfort may be sought in conducting a grand funeral with an expensive casket and dozens of beautiful flower arrangements.

Paul is not saying that Christians don't grieve. He simply says they do not "grieve like the rest of men." Of course there is sorrow at a death—one cannot part even for a short time from a loved one without some sad feelings. But because Paul did not want the Thessalonians to grieve without hope like most people, he presented them the facts about the death of Christians and the Lord's coming. At each funeral they could comfort one another with these truths.

He begins with the most basic fact: Jesus died but then rose again, showing his complete power over death. Paul said if they believe this—and he knew they did—then a second point to believe goes hand in hand with it. Jesus promised that his resurrection means we also will rise from death: "Because I live, you also will live" (John 14:19). Therefore, we are confident that when Jesus comes, he will wake us from the sleep of death and bring us to heaven.

What about those believers who are still alive at the coming of the Lord? Will they have an advantage over those who fell asleep in death? Not at all! With the solemn assurance that this is God's own Word to them, Paul tells the Thessalonians that one group will not precede the other.

Encouraging one another with the resurrection

¹⁶**For the Lord himself will come down from heaven, with a loud command, with the voice of the archangel and with the trumpet call of God, and the dead in Christ will rise first.** ¹⁷**After that, we who are still alive and are left will be caught up together with them in the clouds to meet the Lord in the air. And so we will be with the Lord forever.** ¹⁸**Therefore encourage each other with these words.**

Paul spells out just what will happen on that day of the Lord's return. Christ himself will appear coming down. This will be just the reverse of what the disciples saw at Jesus' ascension when they watched him go up until a cloud hid him from their sight.

Jesus' coming will not be in the humble way he came before. Then he was born in the village of Bethlehem, laid in a manger, and wrapped in swaddling clothes. This time his coming will be accompanied with a "loud command." The voice of the archangel will fill the air, and the piercing sound of a trumpet will call the dead from their graves. All this will take place "in a flash, in the twinkling of an eye" (1 Corinthians 15:52).

Some have misunderstood the expression "the dead in Christ will rise first" to mean that the resurrection of the unbelievers will not take place until sometime after the believers have risen. But remember Paul's main point in all this—one group of believers will not precede another group. And in the very next words, Paul emphasizes that it is only *after* the sleeping believers have been raised that the living believers will join them in meeting with the Lord.

We need not think of this happening in terms of hours or even minutes. The believers who are alive won't have to stand cooling their heels until the believers who are raised join them. Just as the resurrection of all the dead will take place "in a flash, in the twinkling of an eye," so in a moment all the believers, living and resurrected, will be reunited with one another. What a joyful scene that will be for all believers who have been parted by death!

Nor will the joy simply be in the reunion of all believers. More important, this whole group will be together with Christ our Lord. All will be "caught up" by the power of God "in the clouds." Why this? Undoubtedly because God is going to subject the earth to fire, as 2 Peter 3:10 states. Before that takes place all believers will be gone from this earth.

Then they will "meet the Lord." No doubt all of us have wondered at some time or other what it was like to meet Jesus when he lived on earth. Here we will not meet with Jesus in his humble state as the God-man on earth but as the glorified God-man who is Lord of heaven and earth. And we will not have to be afraid or ashamed to stand before him. For he is our brother. He will give us new bodies. These bodies will be the same bodies, but they will be without a sinful nature, imperfections, and weaknesses. Ours will be "imperishable" and "spiritual" bodies (1 Corinthians 15:42-44), like that of our risen Savior himself.

Not only will we meet with the Lord, but thereafter "we will be with the Lord forever." Never again will we be parted from one another by death. Eternal joy and peace will be our lot.

Paul closes by urging the Thessalonians to talk about these facts so they might encourage one another in times of bereavement. Do we wonder what we should say to a bereaved fellow believer at the funeral home, or at church before the funeral service, or when leaving the graveside after the committal, or a week or a month or a year after the funeral? Let's not just say, "I'm so sorry!" Unbelievers can also say this kind of thing in their hopeless grief. How much more comforting it is to hear again and again from the lips of fellow believers the simple facts about the dead in Christ and the coming of our Lord: Christ rose and promises us we will rise also; death is but a sleep from which Christ himself will wake us; at his coming all believers will be reunited to meet with Christ and live with him forever.

You don't have to be a pastor to be able to relate these simple truths. We all know them and believe them.

God bless each of us in our times of bereavement with friends to encourage us through these truths! And, as Paul urges, may we also be quick to comfort and encourage others "with these words"!

Christ's coming will be a disaster for many

5 **Now, brothers, about times and dates we do not need to write you, ²for you know very well that the day of the Lord will come like a thief in the night. ³While people are saying, "Peace and safety," destruction will come on them suddenly, as labor pains on a pregnant woman, and they will not escape.**

Many people are very concerned about knowing just when Christ will return. Some religions have even been founded by men or women who said they knew when the Lord's coming would take place. New predictions continue to be put forth by those who overlook what Scripture says about "times and dates."

God has not chosen to reveal the time when Christ will come nor the reason he planned it for when he did. Anyone who says he knows the time contradicts Jesus' words: "No one knows about that day or hour, not even the angels in heaven, nor the Son, but only the Father" (Matthew 24:36). Thereby he also reveals himself as a false prophet, according to Jesus' warning: "At that time if anyone says to you, 'Look, here is the Christ!' or, 'There he is!' do not believe it" (Matthew 24:23).

Paul reminds the Thessalonians that he had instructed them very clearly on this. Playing a guessing game about the Lord's coming is foolishness, because "the day of the Lord will come like a thief in the night." Here Paul uses Jesus' own picture of a thief to emphasize that Christ's coming will be at a time "when you do not expect him" (Matthew 24:44).

It will also be a time of disaster for many. When the end comes, it will catch them unprepared. They won't even be thinking of the Lord's coming, because they don't consider it a possibility. Others will have a false sense of security because they feel this or that special event has to take place first. Like a trap snaps shut on a mouse, the end will come upon these people. And just as a woman who is in labor pains can't escape those pains by changing her mind and deciding she doesn't want to be pregnant, so they will have no chance to turn back.

The appearance of the Lord will be announced in a flash and a twinkling of an eye by the voice of the archangel and a trumpet's blast. Once this has begun there can be no preparations by unbelievers in order to escape their ruin in God's judgment. It will be too late.

Christians are to put on God's spiritual gifts

⁴But you, brothers, are not in darkness so that this day should surprise you like a thief. ⁵You are all sons of the light and sons of the day. We do not belong to the night or to the darkness. ⁶So then, let us not be like others, who are asleep, but let us be alert and self-controlled. ⁷For those who sleep, sleep at night, and those who get drunk, get drunk at night. ⁸But since we belong to the day, let us be self-controlled, putting on faith and love as a breastplate, and the hope of salvation as a helmet.

The people who say, "Peace and safety," are in "darkness." They really don't know what is going on. They ignore the fact that their sins make them enemies of God. They do not have the peace they imagine. They do not realize that their unforgiven sin must bring the judgment of a just God on them. They have a completely false sense of security.

Paul reminds the Thessalonians that they should know better. They had become "sons of the light" and "sons of the day." The expression "sons of" simply expresses a very close relationship with a person or object. For example "sons of the bridegroom" simply means those closely associated with the bridegroom and so can be translated "guests of the bridegroom" (Mark 2:19). The double expression "light" and "day" emphasizes that the Thessalonians had learned so much about the gospel and were so active in spreading it, that they surely were not people who knew or cared little about the Lord's coming. Therefore, it was unthinkable that the Last Day would find them unprepared like those who lived in the darkness of ignorance and unbelief.

To ensure their preparedness, Paul urges the Thessalonians to put a lot of distance between themselves and their unbelieving neighbors. He admonishes them not to be like those people at all. When people go to sleep at night, they are completely unaware of what might be taking place in the world. Likewise an unbeliever is totally unaware of his impending ruin. He is spiritually sound asleep.

Now Paul uses a different picture, that of a drunk. Sometimes people try to drink their problems away. The alcohol dulls their senses, and for a time they become totally unconcerned about those problems. In the spiritual realm there are people who in the night of their unbelief have some inkling of the consequences of the Lord's coming. They know they have a spiritual problem. But their solution is to dull their consciences with some man-made religious brandy or with the wine of the world's pleasures. This does not solve the problem. It only allows them to become unconcerned about it for awhile.

Instead of such spiritual sleep or drunkenness, Paul urges something better. Christians are to "be alert and self-controlled." Rather than being unaware like one who is asleep, Christ wants the believer to be constantly on the watch for his return in glory. And instead of being unconcerned like one who is drunk, Christ wants his followers to await his coming in full possession of their senses. The believer knows all that the Last Day means for him, and he knows it will be a great day for him. Consequently, he does not become indifferent, even though he has been waiting a long time. The end could come at any time.

But how can we be constantly alert and self-controlled? We are spiritually weak and tired. Satan is constantly attacking our faith with all his might, trying to make us even more sluggish. It seems so easy for Satan to draw our minds completely away from Christ's return! We spend our time concentrating on the journey more than on the journey's goal. Life's problems and pleasures, trials and treasures, sorrows and joys consume our interests. How, then, can we keep from falling into the spiritual sleep or drunkenness?

We can be alert and self-controlled by putting on our God-given armor. Roman soldiers of Paul's day were well protected from the enemy's arrows, spears, and swords only if they put on armor. God has provided his believers with similar protection from the arrows and spears of temptation that Satan and his cohorts hurl at us.

God gives us faith, love, and hope as our armor. Faith is the confidence that God will do whatever he promises. Love is faith in action, living each day as an expression of thanks to God for all he has done for us. The hope of salvation is what sustains our faith and love and encourages them to grow. Without the certain hope that we will be raised from death to live eternally in glory, our faith would be meaningless and we would be people who were "to be pitied more than all men" (1 Corinthians 15:17-19).

How does this God-given armor help us remain watchful for our Lord's coming? It surrounds us with the Lord's strength, so we can take our "stand against the devil's schemes" (Ephesians 6:11). It clothes us with the Lord Jesus Christ so that we "do not think about how to gratify the desires" of our sinful nature (Romans 13:14). It enables us to "demolish arguments and every pretension that sets itself up against the knowledge of God" (2 Corinthians 10:5). It shields us with God's power from despairing amid "all kinds of trials" (1 Peter 1:6). In short, this God-given armor supplies us with the spiritual strength we need. When we stand in the power of God and not our own, we won't fall into the spiritual sleep of the world.

A reminder of why Jesus died

⁹For God did not appoint us to suffer wrath but to receive salvation through our Lord Jesus Christ. ¹⁰He died for us so that, whether we are awake or asleep, we may live together with him. ¹¹Therefore encourage one another and build each other up, just as in fact you are doing.

The reason Christians can live in the hope of salvation is given by Paul in a brief statement that beautifully summarizes the entire gospel.

First he reminds us that God did not "appoint us to suffer wrath." That is, it was not God's will or plan that sinful men should be sent to hell and there "suffer" eternally the punishment of his "wrath." No, God wanted to rescue us from the terrible situation we had brought on ourselves by our sins. And God wanted us to "receive" this salvation as a gift of his mercy. All this he accomplished "through our Lord Jesus Christ."

It was this God-man who paid the penalty we deserved for our sins when he died for us. How did God accomplish this substitution of Jesus for us? By a virgin birth God sent his Son into the world so that he might be made like us in every way. Yet in humbling himself in this way, Jesus retained his divine nature. Thus his precious lifeblood would be the atoning sacrifice for the sins of the whole world. In the words of the apostle Peter, "For you know that it was not with perishable things such as silver or gold that you were redeemed . . . but with the precious blood of Christ, a lamb without blemish or defect" (1 Peter 1:18,19). And as Saint John wrote, "He is the atoning sacrifice for our sins, and not only for ours but also for the sins of the whole world" (1 John 2:2).

Jesus did this, Paul says, both for those who are "awake" and those who are "asleep." These terms might simply refer to Christians who are physically alert or sleeping when Christ comes. Or the terms might refer to believers and unbelievers—Christ died for all. This writer prefers the latter interpretation.

Some think back to Paul's discussion of Christ's return (4:13-18). They take the term *awake* to refer to Christians who are alive at that time and *asleep* to refer to those who have died prior to judgment day. This is unlikely because it ignores the use of these words in the immediate context. Nor is the Greek word *asleep* here the same one used in chapter 4.

The words *awake* and *asleep* are the same as those used for believers who are "alert" and for unbelievers who are "asleep" in regard to Christ's return. So Paul is saying that Jesus died for all people whether they look forward to his second coming or not.

The fact that Christ died for all people doesn't mean that unbelievers will someday live together with him in heaven along with the believers. Because the unbeliever rejects what Christ accomplished for him by his death, he also loses the ultimate goal, namely, eternal life in heaven. Paul reminds the Thessalonians what a waste it would be if they were found asleep, unprepared for their Lord's coming. Then they would lose all that Christ had won for them. In this poignant way Paul uses the gospel to motivate the Thessalonians to put on the spiritual armor that God had given them.

Paul wants them to encourage one another just as he has done—with the gospel. By speaking about the purpose of Christ's death, they would prepare one another for his return. They would also uplift their fellow believers in their troubles. He urges them to do this one-on-one as the Greek implies. This urging is not meant to imply that they hadn't been doing it, but it was intended to have them do it even more.

Surely as members of a Christian congregation, we treasure the family of fellow believers with which God has blessed us. What a joy it is to gather for worship and encourage one another in our faith! We study the message of Christ our Savior. Together we sing the words of the liturgy and hymns. We pray for one another. What a comfort in time of bereavement to have this spiritual family! They remind us of the hope that is ours even as we lay into a grave the body of a loved one who has fallen asleep in Christ!

But members of a family do not speak to one another only when they are gathered as a group. They also do a lot of one-on-one speaking. Twice in this section Paul urges us to do the same as members of a spiritual family: "encourage one another and build each other up." We have such a glorious comfort to share. We share the hope of our Lord's coming. We need to remind one another of this hope, lest we fall asleep and be caught unprepared! How could we possibly not do what the apostle urges?

PART SIX

Final Instructions
(5:12-28)

Hold spiritual leaders in high regard

¹²Now we ask you, brothers, to respect those who work hard among you, who are over you in the Lord and who admonish you. ¹³Hold them in the highest regard in love because of their work. Live in peace with each other.

God wants every group of believers to have a faithful and qualified spiritual leader. He also wants believers to obey and follow the spiritual leader he gives them.

Paul reminds the Thessalonians of these truths about their pastors and teachers. He urges them to take note of the hard work their leaders did for them. It was a temptation for congregations in those days—as it is today—to criticize their ministers. Some people say that a minister's life is an easy one, because he seldom if ever has to do any heavy lifting or other physically strenuous work. All he has to do is stand up and talk—an "hour a week," they say.

Indeed, one hears now and then of a lazy pastor who does try to get by with as little as possible. He neglects the long hours of study or the endless ministering to individuals and small groups that are necessary if he is to be a good shepherd of his flock. But the faithful pastor will be one who works hard among his people, as Paul states.

Paul mentions two things in particular as making up this hard work. One is the position of leadership that God wants a pastor to carry out. For the minister, being "over" people "in the Lord" involves many very important tasks. It means guarding each member of the flock from attacks on his or her faith. It means feeding the flock regularly with an inspiring and edifying message from God's Word. It means a continual study of God's Word so that he does not mislead people but always teaches them God's truth correctly. It means instructing God's people and leading them to do works of service for our Savior. In short, it means providing leadership in all the activities of the Christian congregation: worship, education, evangelism, fellowship, and stewardship.

Second, Paul speaks of the pastor's work of admonishing as hard work. Perhaps this is the hardest work of all. When Christians do not regularly hear God's Word or partake of the Lord's Supper, when quarrels arise between members, when young or old begin to live contrary to God's will in the matter of marriage or sex, when—the list could go on for all those times when Christians need admonition—it is the pastor's work to counsel and to warn in each case. Oh, yes, laypeople can and should encourage and admonish one another also. Paul had emphasized this several times earlier in this letter. Yet the pastor is called by the congregation to be its special spiritual shepherd. By virtue of his training and continued study he is to bring the whole counsel of God to bear on each situation. This is difficult work. Even Christians do not always appreciate the love and concern expressed for their souls' welfare in such personal admonition. Often a pastor is resented for the correction he offers from God's Word. Nevertheless, it is his solemn and important duty to do so.

The word translated "respect" might better be rendered "take note." Paul urges the people to take note of their pastors' work. Then, he continues, "Hold them in the highest regard in love," and this, "because of their work." If people in a congregation fasten their attention on outward matters such as a pastor's personality, appearance, or speaking ability, they often can find something to criticize. This is not to say these things are unimportant. If there is a weakness that hinders his ministry, a faithful pastor will want to remove that weakness.

But notice what Paul wants us to focus on, namely, the work our pastor does, the work of preaching and teaching God's Word. If we remember and appreciate the work our pastor faithfully carries out for our spiritual welfare, we will not honor him with empty words but with deepest Christian love.

Paul now adds, "Live in peace with each other." A lack of peace in a congregation will make the pastor's labor difficult or even impossible. More than that, it will also hinder doing any mission work in the community. When Christians are at odds with one another, their hearts will not be very receptive to the gospel. For their very lives are a denial of the gospel message of love and forgiveness. And which person in the community will be receptive to the gospel from a bickering congregation? Christ's love, which the gospel proclaims, is inevitably overshadowed by any disharmony among those people who claim to be Christians.

So, for the sake of those within and without the church, "Live at peace with each other."

Practice Christian love

¹⁴And we urge you, brothers, warn those who are idle, encourage the timid, help the weak, be patient with everyone. ¹⁵Make sure that nobody pays back wrong for wrong, but always try to be kind to each other and to everyone else.

A pastor's work is to encourage and admonish. Yet the members of a congregation can also do much to correct and help one another.

Earlier in the letter, Paul had urged the Thessalonians not to refuse manual labor as some Greek men did, but to "work with your hands . . . so that you will not be dependent on anybody" (4:11,12). If anyone continued to live the idle life of a loafer, the members of the congregation were to warn him that he was living in sin. Paul's second letter to the Thessalonians indicates that even after a warning was given, some didn't listen. What the congregation was to do in such cases is spelled out in detail in 2 Thessalonians chapter 3.

Some of the members were "timid," that is fainthearted, depressed, or discouraged. Two things mentioned earlier in the letter might have been the cause—persecution and bereavement. But no matter what the cause, Paul urges the members of the congregation to speak words of consolation and encouragement to those whose spirits were nearly broken and who were ready to give up.

Another way to practice Christian love is to lend a helping hand to those who are weak because of some bodily illness or disability. Literally the word *help* means "to hold on to." People with bodily ailments of any kind have a special burden to bear. They need the help of Christian brothers and sisters in bearing that burden, and every helping hand we lend is not only much appreciated by the "weak" but is also noted by Christ as if we did it for him. In Matthew 25:40 he states, "I tell you the truth, whatever you did for one of the least of these brothers of mine, you did for me."

Patience with others is a fruit of faith. The Lord's long-suffering patience toward us in all our sins and weaknesses is a daily experience. Our fellow Christians have weaknesses and characteristics that may at times irritate us. God's love in Christ provides us with the patience we need to live and work in a congregation with them.

Moreover, Paul shows that our patience goes beyond our fellow Christians to "everyone." God in his patience does not strike the unbeliever down immediately but gives him a longer time of grace to repent. We who by grace already live in repentance are motivated thereby to practice that same patience.

Revenge is a powerful motivating force in the heart of every person because of the pride and selfishness of the sinful nature with which we were born. When we are wronged by someone, therefore, our natural inclination is to get even by paying back "wrong for wrong." But what is natural for our sinful nature is opposed by the new spirit created in us by the Holy Spirit. Instead of revenge, this new spirit leads us to follow our Savior's instructions to love our enemies and to do good to those who sin against us.

But this new spirit is often weak, and the sinful nature easily gets the upper hand in moments of weakness. Therefore Paul wants us to be concerned about one another in this matter.

If we see a brother or sister seeking revenge, we should "make sure" to help him or her put down the old Adam and stop trying to pay back "wrong for wrong."

Instead, God wants us to "try to be kind." "Try to" does not mean something like "Well, I tried, but I find it hard to do." It means try in the sense that we earnestly pursue something as a constant way of life. Only Christ's love for us can motivate us to such lives of kindness. Ephesians 4:32 says it best: "Be kind and compassionate to one another, forgiving each other, just as in Christ God forgave you."

Pattern your whole life after God's will

[16]Be joyful always; [17]pray continually; [18]give thanks in all circumstances, for this is God's will for you in Christ Jesus. [19]Do not

put out the Spirit's fire; ²⁰do not treat prophecies with contempt. ²¹Test everything. Hold on to the good. ²²Avoid every kind of evil.

In rapid fire no less than eight imperatives follow one after the other. With eight commands Paul reviews for us what "God's will" for us is "in Christ Jesus." These are not man-made guidelines. They are from God himself. The world may scoff at many of these guidelines as being non-sense, or as being impossible, or as restricting one's free-dom too much. For those who are "in Christ Jesus," they are vital and the way of true freedom and happiness.

It might seem impossible to live a life in which one is "joyful always." It is easy to be joyful in good times, but what about all the trials and tribulations that cause us sorrow?

For the person who belongs to Christ by faith there is joy even in sorrow. Why? Because believers know that Christ rules heaven and earth, so the sorrow that enters our lives is not a matter of blind fate. Anything that causes us sorrow is something our Savior permitted to come only to serve our good. Sorrows draw us closer to him (Romans 5:3-5); they purify our faith like gold is refined in fire (1 Peter 1:7); they provide us with opportunities to confess before others the hope that is in us (1 Peter 3:13-15). There is, however, one thing sorrow cannot do. It can never, never separate us from God's love (Romans 8:39). God's Spirit helps us and prays for us in our weaknesses. And we know God will keep his promises to watch over us and care for us in our sorrows.

So we can "consider it pure joy . . . whenever [we] face trials" (James 1:2). There was little in the early Christian church in which most people today would find much joy. The believers were persecuted. Most of them were poor. Still those early Christians had a joy in Christ that nothing and no one could take away.

It might also seem impossible, and even nonsensical, to most people that one should "pray continually." How can a person pray nonstop without taking time out at least to eat and to sleep?

When Paul urges constant prayer, he is not suggesting that we sit at all times with hands folded and heads bowed in conscious prayer. The Christian either consciously or unconsciously commits all things at all times to him who cares for us. When this is the inward spirit of a person by faith, he will also express it outwardly in words of petition, praise, and thanks.

Often we are quick to ask God for things we need but then forget to thank him when he answers our request. Ten lepers came to Jesus asking to be healed. Only one returned to give thanks! May Jesus' sad question "Where are the nine?" (Luke 17:17) remind us how pleased he is to receive our thanks. Let us never forget to thank him for all his blessings.

Nor is our thankfulness limited to words. We can also express it "in all circumstances" by our actions. "Whatever you do," Paul writes in Colossians 3:17, "whether in word or deed, do it all in the name of the Lord Jesus, giving thanks to God the Father through him." The Christian mother who cares for her children, cleans the house, cooks meals, and mends clothes is expressing her thanks to God in all these actions. Since she does them as a child of God who rejoices in her Savior, her simplest task is an act of faith, which God looks on as an expression of true gratitude. That's how it is with the simplest actions of every Christian, whether a laborer, farmer, businessperson, clerk, police officer, or secretary. Whether we eat or drink—whatever we do—God wants us to do it all to his glory. That is how we "give thanks in all circumstances."

Next Paul instructs, "Do not put out the Spirit's fire." The fire the Spirit starts in us is the fire of faith. Our coming to faith is a miracle in which we have no part. But once we believe, we have a new man in us who enables us to fight "the good fight" of faith (2 Timothy 4:7) and to "work out [our] salvation with fear and trembling" (Philippians 2:12) in cooperation with God's Holy Spirit.

God wants us to "crucify" the sinful nature with its passions and desires and "keep in step with the Spirit" (Galatians 5:25). To this end God gives us the means of grace: the Bible and the sacraments of Baptism and the Lord's Supper. Through these means the Holy Spirit strengthens our faith and renews our zeal to live according to the new man. Failure to make use of the Word and sacraments, then, would by default give the old Adam the upper hand and thus put out the Spirit's fire.

This Paul underscores by the next admonition. The term *prophecies* refers to God's revealed Word. A prophet is simply one who speaks a message from God to man. The Bible is made up of numerous prophecies, which God gave "at many times and in various ways" (Hebrews 1:1).

The word translated "to treat with contempt" also means "to empty of all authority." Used with the word *prophecies* it points to a refusal to recognize the words of Scripture as the inspired words of God. Many today consider the doctrine of verbal inspiration impossible and nonsensical. They treat much of the Bible with contempt by putting it on a par with man's word. They disregard verses, chapters, and whole books as they choose. Paul urges us never to do what they do, lest God's punishment spoken of in Revelation 22:18,19 fall upon us: "I warn everyone who hears the words of the prophecy of this book: If anyone adds anything to them, God will add to him the plagues described in this book. And if anyone takes words away from this book of prophecy, God will take away from him his share in the tree of life and in the holy city, which are described in this book."

The Christian life is a life of constant testing, the apostle adds. The word *test* is the Greek word used for testing the genuineness of such things as gold and silver. If there were any impurities in these precious metals, they failed the test. The standard God wants us to use is his pure Word. The Christian is to test "everything" in this way. "Everything" includes all that is taught as the will of God (law) and all that is proclaimed about God's goodness and mercy (gospel). We are to be on constant lookout for any human impurities that might be brought into the precious truths God has revealed. Everything we meet in our daily lives is to be examined in the light of God's Word.

Once we have tested for genuineness, we are to act upon what we have found. If we have found that what we are testing is "good" according to the standard of God's Word, then we are to "hold on to" it. The final judgment we make is not to be based on whether something works or whether it may bring about some seemingly good results but only on whether or not it is in full accord with Scripture. On good things we are to get such a firm hold that no one can pry us loose.

On the other hand, if we find that something is "evil" by its nature, we are to "avoid" it. The word *avoid* literally means "to hold oneself far away." Consciously and constantly God wants us to put a lot of distance between ourselves and whatever conflicts, even in a small way, with his pure Word. Why? Because "a little yeast works through the whole batch of dough" (Galatians 5:9). A little bit of impurity mixed with God's truth will eventually destroy the truth and lead to one error after another.

Note that Paul stresses the avoiding of "every kind" of evil. We are to shun not just one kind of evil but every form of impurity that Satan can come up with.

65

It is a formidable list of commands that Paul has penned here by inspiration of the Spirit. One writer has called them the jewels that crown a Christian's life. They are guidelines that God urges upon us for our good both now and eternally. Read them once more—slowly—and let them be impressed on your mind so that you remember them. Then with the Lord's help go out and live them!

Closing prayer, greeting, benediction

[23]May God himself, the God of peace, sanctify you through and through. May your whole spirit, soul and body be kept blameless at the coming of our Lord Jesus Christ. [24]The one who calls you is faithful and he will do it.

[25]Brothers, pray for us. [26]Greet all the brothers with a holy kiss. [27]I charge you before the Lord to have this letter read to all the brothers.

[28]The grace of our Lord Jesus Christ be with you.

Earlier in the letter Paul had reminded the Thessalonians that their pastors would encourage them to live according to God's will. He also urged the Thessalonians to help one another in sanctified living. Now he prays that "God himself" would sanctify them. The prayer that closes this letter doesn't imply that their pastors and fellow members were ineffectual in their efforts. It simply asks God, from whom all blessings flow, to bless every effort to help them grow in holy living.

Paul prays that God might sanctify them "through and through." In Ephesians 4:13 the goal of Christian growth is described in words expressing the same thought: "attaining to the whole measure of the fullness of Christ." That is a level of sanctification we can never reach in this life. But "Christ's love compels us" (2 Corinthians 5:14) to be satisfied with nothing less. Paul had given them many instructions in this letter about living God-pleasing lives.

Paul prays that God, who established that glorious peace between all people and himself, would continually help the Thessalonians grow in sanctification toward that goal.

Second, Paul prays that God would keep them in faith without falling backward in any way so that they would be blameless at the Lord's coming. Only the believer who by faith is clothed in Jesus' blood and righteousness will be found blameless when Christ comes to judge the living and the dead. By adding up the terms "spirit, soul, and body" and putting the adjective "whole" before these three, Paul emphasizes how earnestly he prays that God will keep them faithful to the end. We remember how concerned Paul was that the persecution might have led them to abandon Christ. We know that one of the chief purposes of this letter was to encourage and strengthen them even more, now that he knew they were standing firm. This prayer, then, is a fitting conclusion to everything he has written.

And Paul is sure the Lord will hear his prayers. After all, God is faithful. God often promises in his Word that he will send his Holy Spirit to strengthen his dear children in their faith and in their desire to live lives of thanks to him. Because God is faithful, he never fails to do what he promises. That's why Paul could assure the Thessalonians, "He will do it."

Paul also asks the Thessalonians to pray for him and Silas and Timothy. They were in Corinth at this time, preaching the gospel with great success but also meeting with many disappointments and strong opposition. Just as he knew they needed and appreciated his prayers for them, so he wanted them to know how much he needed and appreciated their prayers on his behalf.

He tells them to greet all the fellow Christians in Thessalonica with "a holy kiss." A kiss was a common greeting of friendship in Jesus' day. It was, we recall, with a kiss that

67

Judas betrayed Jesus. Paul calls the kiss of greeting among Christians "holy," because it expressed that special friendship that was theirs as members of God's holy family in Christ.

He urges, finally, that the Thessalonians should make sure this letter is read to every believer. With the words "I charge you before the Lord," Paul puts them under solemn oath to do what he directs.

Why is Paul so concerned that the exact words of his letter be read to every believer? The reason readily suggests itself. This is no ordinary letter, but one written by the inspiration of God. That is exactly the way the apostle Peter describes all Paul's letters, when he states, "Our dear brother Paul also wrote you with the wisdom that God gave him" (2 Peter 3:15). Since all of God's Word is vital for believers' growth in knowledge, faith, and sanctification, Paul could not just leave it to chance that somehow they might hear about this letter.

This letter was either the first or second that Paul wrote. (See the Introduction.) Therefore, it gives a clear instruction what is to be done with all subsequent inspired letters. They were not just to be read by a select few but by all believers.

Did the people restrict the reading of this letter to believers within Thessalonica? That is unlikely. Rather, just as they had been like a bell ringing God's Word throughout the whole country and beyond, so they must have let this divine letter ring out also. When Peter wrote the passage referred to above, this letter (as all Paul's letters) had reached Asia Minor and was well known there also.

Paul's benediction is a standard but beautiful one. Everything we are, and everything we will be in eternity, is a result of God's grace. When the apostle speaks this blessing, he could ask for nothing more precious: "The grace of our Lord Jesus Christ be with you."

Sometimes in our haste we skip over the personal prayers, greetings, and benedictions at the end of Paul's letters. We shouldn't. Here too are important lessons for us to learn.

What better prayer could we pray than that which Paul prayed for the Thessalonians' growth in sanctified living and for their being kept blameless until Christ's coming? What more encouraging words could we hear than Paul's reminder that God is faithful? He will keep all his gracious promises to us.

The request of Paul that the Thessalonians pray for him and his companions surely reminds us to pray for pastors and missionaries. Paul's encouragement to the Thessalonians to extend a special greeting to their fellow believers shows us how important it is to express the oneness of faith we share with all the members of our spiritual family.

The solemn charge that every believer read this letter impresses on us how important it is to read and hear the exact words of Scripture. We ought not be satisfied to hear about them in some secondhand way. The benediction Paul wrote is one we often hear our pastor speak. Let us appreciate it for the matchless blessing it is!

Truly, 1 Thessalonians is an inspiring yet down-to-earth, doctrinal yet very practical, letter. As we treasure it, may we grow in faith and holy living, just as Paul prayed for all who read it!

Introduction to 2 Thessalonians

Setting, occasion, and purpose

Since Paul sent this letter to the same congregation as 1 Thessalonians, everything we said in the introduction to that letter about the historical setting applies here as well. All we need to add is the time and place from which he wrote this second epistle.

It seems Paul was still in Corinth when he composed 2 Thessalonians because Silas and Timothy were with him, just as when he had written the first letter. It would be difficult to find a time after Paul left Corinth and completed his second mission journey when we could say with certainty that these two companions were together with Paul again.

The fact that Paul most likely wrote from Corinth also suggests that he wrote 2 Thessalonians only a matter of months after the first letter. After Paul had sent that first letter, news came from Thessalonica about several matters that required a follow-up letter. How the news came we don't know. But since Thessalonica and Corinth were both important crossroads cities, it is not hard to understand that news traveled from one city to the other and back again within a few weeks' time.

Author

As in the first letter, Paul mentions Silas and Timothy as coauthors. Throughout the letter the plurals *we* or *us* or *our* occur.

Just as in 1 Thessalonians, however, there are several places (2:5; 3:17) in which the singular *I* is used. This indicates that Paul again is the primary author. The two companions' recent connections with the Thessalonians would explain why Silas and Timothy would join Paul in expressing the thoughts that this letter contains.

Summary

Paul addresses three distinct matters in this letter, two of which he treated in his first epistle. He again speaks of the fierce persecution by the Jews and of the Thessalonians' faithfulness.

Taking off from these topics, Paul raises a new point that has to do with Christ's return. When Christ Jesus comes in judgment, the tables will be turned. Then the persecutors will be the troubled ones, while the persecuted will have relief because they will be glorified. This added fact about Jesus' coming would encourage the Thessalonians even more in their trials.

In 1 Thessalonians Paul had also spoken about not being idle. He had urged the Thessalonians to support themselves. In spite of this apostolic admonition, some members of the church continued to sponge off others and refused to work. Now Paul urges the congregation to take disciplinary action against those who were persisting in this sin. He cites his own example of working to provide for himself when he was among the Thessalonians, even though he could have rightly expected support from them. He declares that those who refuse to work shouldn't be given any help.

The suggestion is often made that these people were idle only because they had the mistaken notion that Christ's second coming was imminent. And, consequently, they didn't need to do anything except wait for that day. There are a number of reasons why this suggestion is not compelling. First, in his preceding letter Paul's treatment of working was not related to his discussion of Christ's second coming. Rather, he urged the people to work as an application of the principle of brotherly love. Second, the section of 2 Thessalonians that precedes the warning against idleness does not necessarily address itself to a misunderstanding that Christ's coming was imminent. Instead, the mistaken notion might very well have been that Christ had *already* come. Finally, if their idleness had been connected with an eager anticipation for Christ's second coming, Paul might at least have commended them for their eagerness, while at the same time urging them to rid their waiting of this one false conclusion.

The reason for their idleness was more likely the inclination of Greek men to avoid manual labor. We mentioned this in our comments on 1 Thessalonians 4:11,12. Paul had thoroughly discussed this subject when he was in Thessalonica. In the first letter, he speaks of it as a teaching on which they were very well informed. In that letter he again admonished them about idleness. Therefore, in this letter he emphasizes that persisting in this sin could not be tolerated after his third admonition. "In the name of the Lord Jesus Christ," Paul asserts, "we command you, brothers, to keep away from every brother who is idle and does not live according to the teaching you received from us" (3:6).

The most famous part of 2 Thessalonians deals with something Paul hadn't mentioned in his first letter, the coming of the Antichrist. Paul calls him "the man of lawlessness." All of chapter 2 and the first part of chapter 3 discuss this subject. Of Paul's two letters to the Thessalonians, no other teaching has been subject to so much misinterpretation and speculation. As we shall see, however, when we study these verses as a whole (rather than isolating any part from the rest), they clearly establish the Roman Catholic papacy as the historical fulfillment of this prophetic description.

Outline

A. God's just judgment on persecutors (1:1-12)
1. Thanksgiving for the Thessalonians' faith and perseverance (1:1-4)
2. Relief for those who suffer for God's kingdom (1:5-7)
3. God will punish the persecutor (1:8-10)
4. Paul prays for the Thessalonians to glorify Jesus (1:11,12)
B. The prophecy of the Antichrist (2:1–3:5)
1. The Antichrist will be revealed (2:1-3)
2. The rise and fall of the Antichrist (2:4-8)
3. Satan uses the Antichrist to damn people (2:9-12)
4. Paul thanks God that the Thessalonians follow Christ (2:13,14)
5. Paul urges the Thessalonians to stand firm (2:15-17)
6. Paul asks for the Thessalonians' prayers and assures them of God's protection (3:1-5)
C. Disciplining a brother in the sin of idleness (3:6-18)
1. Paul urges separation from those who live off others (3:6-9)
2. Idleness is contrary to Christ's will (3:10-13)
3. Discipline should seek to win back a brother (3:14,15)
4. Closing prayer, greeting, benediction (3:16-18)

PART ONE

God's Just Judgment on Persecutors
(1:1-12)

Thanksgiving for the Thessalonians' faith and perseverance

1 Paul, Silas and Timothy,
To the church of the Thessalonians in God our Father and the Lord Jesus Christ: ²Grace and peace to you from God the Father and the Lord Jesus Christ. ³We ought always to thank God for you, brothers, and rightly so, because your faith is growing more and more, and the love every one of you has for each other is increasing. ⁴Therefore, among God's churches we boast about your perseverance and faith in all the persecutions and trials you are enduring.

The opening verse of this letter is almost identical with that of the first letter. The only change—and it is not a significant one—is the pronoun *our* in place of *the* before *Father*.

Paul again includes Silas and Timothy with himself as the ones from whom his letter is coming. Then, as was the custom in letters at that time, the apostle states to whom the letter is written.

In the same words as in the first letter, Paul describes the Thessalonians as being "in" the Father and "in" Jesus. This wording emphasizes that they did not have some loose connection with God but that God had drawn them very close to himself. In spite of persecution, they were safely in the realm of God's loving care.

The triple name of God's Son emphasizes three distinct and important things about him. He is "Lord"—true God. He is "Jesus"—Savior from sin. He is "Christ"—the one chosen by God to be our Prophet, Priest, and King.

Paul greets the Thessalonians with his usual two words: *grace* and *peace.* Though simple they are filled with boundless meaning. God's grace, or undeserved love, is the only cause of our salvation. We have done nothing to deserve anything from God. Peace is the result of our salvation. We are no longer enemies of God who must live in constant dread of him. We are his dear children. Grace and peace—what greater blessings could anyone ask for fellow believers?

Apparently the news about the Thessalonians that came to Paul in the intervening month or months since he had written the first letter was for the most part very good. The Thessalonians had continued to bear up under the persecution and to grow in faith and love. When we remember how bitter the persecution was that they were suffering at the hands of unbelieving Jews, their continued spiritual growth was an astounding development.

Their faith in Christ their Savior never wavered, even though this was the reason the Jews hated and attacked them. Each bit of news that came to Paul indicated they had grown even more in faith since the last time he heard about them. They placed themselves confidently into God's hands, knowing he would either end the persecution or help them bear it. The Thessalonians were not going to deny Christ just to escape this trial. Rather, they were constantly seeking new ways to spread the message of the Savior.

In his first letter Paul had urged them to put their faith into action by showing love to one another and to all people. This they did. It wasn't just most of the believers who did this, but, says Paul, "every one" of them.

What a marvelous congregation the Thessalonians had! Oh, they were sinners—imperfect people like us. But in

Christlike love they forgave one another their sins and weaknesses. They shared their unity in faith in an atmosphere of love. Instead of causing them to turn on one another, their trials drew them closer together. They offered loving help to any needy or distressed member of their spiritual family.

It was amazing that "every one" of them had such love "for each other." Equally amazing were the reports that Paul received that their love was constantly "increasing."

This growth in faith and love was not something the Thessalonians accomplished on their own. Yes, they had continued to make faithful use of the Word and sacraments as Paul had urged. But it was the Holy Spirit who had continued to work through those means of grace to bring about the growth. To emphasize this point, Paul tells the Thessalonians that every time he heard a good report about them he spoke a prayer of thanks to God.

When Paul says that he "ought" to thank God, he does not mean something like, "I ought to do it, but it seems I never get around to it." The word here expresses the idea of an obligation, a debt that must be paid. Paul's joy in what God was doing placed him under obligation to thank God continually for these blessings. Nor did Paul look at this "obligation" as a grievous burden. It was a duty he carried out with joy.

In addition to thanking God for this blessing, Paul also spoke to other Christian congregations about the Thessalonians' spiritual growth. What an inspiring example the Thessalonians were for all other Christians of that day—and ours! The Thessalonians suffered trials of every sort: illnesses, bereavements, poverty, disappointments, severe persecution. Yet they endured all this with a model God-given perseverance and faith.

When Paul says he "boasted" about this to the other congregations, he is glorifying neither the Thessalonians nor his own achievements. He is glorifying God. It was to God and him alone that Paul owed a continuing debt of thanks for what was accomplished in Thessalonica.

What could be the purpose of glorifying God by this "boast"? Really there were two purposes. One was to encourage other congregations in their trials and persecutions by the example of the heroic Thessalonians. The other was to encourage the Thessalonians themselves, by assuring them that their heroic struggle was not forgotten. In fact, their tribulations were known among Christians everywhere. The Thessalonians could take heart in the awareness that their fellow believers would be offering many, many prayers in their behalf.

This section contains two significant lessons for us. One is the ability God gives us, like the Thessalonians, to grow in faith and love, even in times of trouble. When troubles come, God doesn't intend for us to despair and weaken in faith. Rather, he wants us to listen all the more closely to his Word. Then he will strengthen us to bear our trials, and he will increase our love for each other so we help one another in time of need. God wants us also to bring all our cares to him in prayer "because he cares" for us (1 Peter 5:7). The beloved hymn "What a Friend We Have in Jesus" was written in the aftermath of personal tragedy. The author, Joseph Scriven, lost his bride-to-be when she met with a boating accident and drowned the day before their wedding. From his personal tragedy he turned to God in prayer. We too can learn to bring all our cares to the Lord.

> What a friend we have in Jesus,
> All our sins and griefs to bear!
> What a privilege to carry
> Ev'rything to God in prayer!
> Oh, what peace we often forfeit,

>Oh, what needless pain we bear,
>All because we do not carry
>Ev'rything to God in prayer! (CW 411:1)

Second, God wants the "boasting" that our missionaries do about the "perseverance and faith" of believers in other parts of the world to inspire us. When a missionary talks about how believers elsewhere suffer shame and loss for Jesus' sake, it does not glorify the missionary or those people. It glorifies God, because it is he who gave them such persevering faith. Listen, then, to our missionaries as they cite examples of heroic faith, which God has worked in our fellow believers. And be encouraged in any trials or persecution you might suffer!

Finally, do not forget to pray for those whom God asks to suffer for their faith. We too owe God a debt of thanks for the joy that every report about them gives us. They need our prayers that God will give them faith and love in their difficult situations.

Relief for those who suffer for God's kingdom

⁵All this is evidence that God's judgment is right, and as a result you will be counted worthy of the kingdom of God, for which you are suffering. ⁶God is just: He will pay back trouble to those who trouble you ⁷and give relief to those who are troubled, and to us as well. This will happen when the Lord Jesus is revealed from heaven in blazing fire with his powerful angels.

It is easy for Christians undergoing trials to begin to think that maybe their suffering is a judgment of God on their sins. Paul doesn't want the Thessalonians to think this way, so he now speaks about the two sides of God's judgment. At the same time God judges the wicked worthy of eternal suffering, he also judges the believers worthy of living in his eternal kingdom. In these verses Paul focuses mainly on God's judgment of the believers. A more detailed description of the wicked will follow in the next verses.

Paul had just spoken of their spiritual growth during the persecution and how he had boasted about this. These truths should make it clear to the Thessalonians that their sufferings were not a punishment for sin. They were "evidence" or a demonstration of the double judgment that God would render on the Last Day. Above all, they were a demonstration that the Thessalonians would be judged to be believers.

A similar passage in 1 Peter helps explain how persecution and faithfulness in persecution are evidence that God has declared someone belongs to him. Peter addressed this letter to Christians in Asia Minor. Like the Thessalonians, these people were suffering persecution. He points out that being persecuted for Christ is not something strange but common for Christ's followers. "Dear friends," writes Peter, "do not be surprised at the painful trial you are suffering, as though something strange were happening to you. But rejoice that you participate in the sufferings of Christ. . . . If you are insulted because of the name of Christ, you are blessed, for the Spirit of glory and of God rests on you" (1 Peter 4:12-14). If a person suffers for the name of Christ, then it is proof that he belongs to the Lord. If one did not belong to Christ, one wouldn't suffer for being a Christian.

In short, far from being a punishment for sins, a Christian's persecution is proof that he belongs to Christ. The world will always hate the children of God. These are the truths both Paul and Peter—indeed, the entire Scripture—emphasize.

Paul now summarizes the facts concerning God's double judgment. Since God is just, two things will take place at the end of the world. One will be that he will pay back in kind the trouble that the persecutors brought upon the believers. Their persecution of believers is evidence of their unbelief. In the following verses, Paul will say much more about the terrible "trouble" to come on the unbelieving persecutors. The other thing that will happen because God is just is that the persecuted will find "relief."

When Paul speaks about this "relief," he adds that it will not just come to the Thessalonians but also to Paul, Silas, and Timothy. They too were under constant persecution for their faith in Christ. In other words, everyone who suffered persecution for being a Christian will suffer no more.

The word *relief* is surely an understatement. It states only that the persecution will end. It does not state the wonderful life that will replace life in this persecuting world. But we know from the rest of Scripture that heaven is not simply a place free from trouble. It is also a place where happiness is guaranteed and never ending. What a wonderful relief that will be for every Christian, especially the persecuted.

God has set the day for this twofold judgment to take place. It will happen when Jesus comes in glory. We do not know when that day will be. But it will surely come, and suddenly "the Lord Jesus [will be] revealed from heaven." Now Jesus fills heaven and earth with his invisible presence. Then he will reveal himself visibly to all people. He will come "with his powerful angels." In Jesus' name they will carry out all that needs to be done on that day. According to the book of Revelation, this includes such tasks as gathering all people before Christ's judgment throne and destroying the earth.

The words "in blazing fire" signal the punishing wrath of Christ when he comes. It is this second aspect of Christ's judgment to which Paul now addresses himself in more detail.

God will punish the persecutor

[8]He will punish those who do not know God and do not obey the gospel of our Lord Jesus. [9]They will be punished with everlasting destruction and shut out from the presence of the Lord and from the majesty of his power [10]on the day he comes to be glorified in his holy people and to be marveled at among all those who have believed. This includes you, because you believed our testimony to you.

The persecutor will see Christ coming as one dressed "in blazing fire." Christ holds back his punishment of these wicked men until the end of the world lest in punishing them he also harm his beloved followers. So he lets the "weeds" grow among the "wheat" until it's time for the harvest. Then, as Jesus puts it in his parable, "At that time I will tell the harvesters: First collect the weeds and tie them in bundles to be burned; then gather the wheat and bring it into my barn" (Matthew 13:30). So the fire of God's anger will blaze against the unbelievers.

Two separate groups will be punished. First, those who did not "know God"; that is, who did not acknowledge him as God. All people can clearly learn some things about God from his creation, namely, his eternal power, his wisdom, and his divine nature. But most people do not want to acknowledge this. They suppress this truth by their wickedness. Their foolish hearts are darkened. They worship idols and revel in sins that they know deserve punishment. For this refusal to acknowledge what they know about God from creation, Christ in blazing fire will punish them.

The second group is those who, although they knew the true God not only as the God of creation but also as the

Savior-God, refused to believe that it was by Christ's redeeming work alone that they are righteous. In various ways they insisted on adding something they did to what Christ had already completed for them, and so they denied Christ. This is what Paul means when he says that they "do not obey the gospel of our Lord Jesus." The gospel tells us that everything is done for our salvation and, therefore, we are not to try to add anything, otherwise "grace would no longer be grace" (Romans 11:6).

The Thessalonians undoubtedly caught the fact that the Jews who were persecuting them fit into this second group. It was the particular sin of the unbelieving Jews that although they were God's chosen people, they disregarded the righteousness that God provided them in Christ. Instead they sought to establish their own righteousness. In this they were guilty of not submitting to, or not obeying, the gospel. Since Paul is speaking in broad terms here of God's final judgment, he is referring not only to those persecuting Jews in Thessalonica but to all who follow their fatal self-righteous error.

The punishment that Christ will bring in blazing fire upon both these groups will be the same. The penalty they will pay will be "everlasting destruction." This seems at first to be a contradiction. How can something be destroyed and yet be everlasting? But that will be the terrible agony of those upon whom God's just judgment will fall. They will be going through the process of destruction in the fire of hell, but that process will never end. They will wish for their own annihilation, but their wishes will not be granted.

Their agony will be especially this, namely, their complete separation from "the presence of the Lord and from the majesty of his power." While the believers enjoy God's loving presence and bask in the light of his majesty, the unbelievers will never see God's glory or have any hope of seeing it through all eternity. What a terrible punishment these few words describe!

So that the Thessalonians do not forget that God's judgment is twofold, Paul returns to the positive side of that judgment. On the day Christ comes like a blazing fire for the unbelieving, and especially for the persecutors—on that same day, Christ will come in an entirely different way for the believers, especially the persecuted believers.

He will come "to be glorified in his holy people." Christ is the head; the believers are his body. He came to redeem them so they might be with him eternally. Without them with him in heaven, his plan of salvation would not be complete.

Christ Jesus will come with a loud command. He will raise the dead and then take all believers to meet him in the air and to be with him forever. When this happens, all the believers will glorify him with their praises and with holy lives.

He will also come "to be marveled at among all those who have believed." Because heaven is so far beyond description for human beings, God tells us really very little of what it will be like. The Bible says there will be no sorrows, only joy. There will be no sin, only righteousness. Our bodies will not be weak or imperfect in any way, but like Jesus' glorious body. From these few facts we know about heaven, we might think we can imagine what it will be like. But when we actually are there with Christ, it will be far beyond anything we could have imagined. "This is too good to be true!" we'll exclaim, as we stand in amazement at what our loving God has provided for us as our eternal home.

Paul assures the Thessalonians that this picture of heaven includes them also, because they believed the testimony he gave them both during his visit to Thessalonica and in the first letter he wrote them. That was why they were persecuted, and, as Paul stated, their growth in faith under persecution was "evidence" they belonged to Christ. God's just judgment on them would be quite different from that on their persecutors.

Paul intended this statement about the twofold judgment of Christ to encourage the Thessalonians. For this same reason the Lord had it recorded in Scripture for us. God's judgment of "everlasting destruction" upon the persecutors is not intended for us to gloat over their punishment. Instead, these words are to remind us that although God may allow us to suffer severe persecution, he is still in charge. A day of reckoning is surely coming. Persecutors will pay the penalty for their opposition to the gospel. Knowing that God is in control strengthens and encourages us to bear up with patient endurance even in the darkest of days.

On the other hand, the certainty that we shall be judged worthy of heaven is not intended to make us complacent. The evidence that we are Christ's, which is supplied by anything we suffer for his name's sake, also strengthens us in the troubles of our earthly lives. We belong to Christ. We will be among the holy believers who will glorify Christ and marvel at his goodness when he is revealed from heaven with his powerful angels. This knowledge does not make us gloat. Rather, it encourages us in the severest of troubles to continue to fight the good fight of faith until we receive this promised crown of glory.

Paul prays for the Thessalonians to glorify Jesus

¹¹With this in mind, we constantly pray for you, that our God may count you worthy of his calling, and that by his power he may fulfill every good purpose of yours and every act prompted by your faith. ¹²We pray this so that the name of our Lord Jesus may be glorified in you, and you in him, according to the grace of our God and the Lord Jesus Christ.

As in his first letter, here again Paul does not want to leave his readers with the impression that Christians remain faithful as a result of their own intentions or abilities. God alone does all this.

When he thinks about the wonderful judgment that God will speak upon all believers on the Last Day, Paul tells the Thessalonians that he prays about it constantly on their behalf. By faith in Jesus the Thessalonians would be declared "worthy of the kingdom of God." To use Martin Luther's words from the Explanation to the Second Article of the Apostles' Creed, God had called them to "live under him in his kingdom, and serve him in everlasting righteousness, innocence, and blessedness." Paul prays that God would make the Thessalonians worthy of this high calling by directing their thoughts and actions.

The new man created in them by God was capable only of good intentions and actions prompted by faith. But their old Adam diametrically opposed such intentions and actions. In this struggle, which goes on in every Christian, the old Adam can easily get the upper hand. He is supported by all the superhuman powers at Satan's command, "the powers of this dark world and . . . the spiritual forces of evil in the heavenly realms" (Ephesians 6:12). Every Christian needs God's help in this daily fight. Quoting Luther again from the Small Catechism, "God . . . breaks and defeats every evil plan and purpose of the devil, the world, and our sinful flesh." Paul prays that God would empower the Thessalonians to live holy lives, filling them with good intentions and with a faith that is active in deeds of love.

This was Paul's prayer because he desired that "the name of our Lord Jesus may be glorified" in them. Every good intention that they would act on would serve to glorify Christ. Why? Because every good deed a Christian performs is done to thank Jesus for all that he did to save us. To fellow believers and to the unbelievers who live around that Christian, his good deeds say one thing, namely, "I love my Savior." Thus the believer's whole life glorifies Christ.

Paul not only prays that Christ will be glorified by the Thessalonians but also that they might be glorified in Christ. By remaining faithful to the end, the Christian is assured of a crown of life, which Christ will give him. Christians confess Christ on earth. When he comes at the end of the world, Christ promises he will in turn confess every Christian before his Father in heaven. In this way Christ will glorify them, even as they now glorify him. Paul prays that the Thessalonians may share in this blessing too.

In closing this section, Paul once again emphasizes that all this comes about only "according to the grace of our God and the Lord Jesus Christ." We do not keep ourselves faithful to Christ until our end. No, it is only because of God's undeserved love, showered on us daily, that this can happen.

As we think about God's final twofold judgment, we will pray for one another as Paul did for the Thessalonians. Our new man is also easily bested by our old Adam. We need to pray for one another that God would enable us to think and act only in those ways that are prompted by our faith. Our purpose in such prayer will also be that Christ's name might be glorified by us and that we someday might be glorified by him. How could our purpose be any different? We remember that all this is made possible by his grace and not by our merit.

May God move us to such prayer for one another! Let's pray especially for those who must suffer persecution as Christians.

PART TWO

The Prophecy of the Antichrist
(2:1–3:5)

The Antichrist will be revealed

2 **Concerning the coming of our Lord Jesus Christ and our being gathered to him, we ask you, brothers, ²not to become easily unsettled or alarmed by some prophecy, report or letter supposed to have come from us, saying that the day of the Lord has already come. ³Don't let anyone deceive you in any way, for that day will not come until the rebellion occurs and the man of lawlessness is revealed, the man doomed to destruction.**

When people think about the end of the world, it often seems they are ready to believe any rumor that comes along. This happens especially when people have not carefully studied what God says about that awesome day. It seems that some of the Thessalonians were no different. A false notion about the end of the world was circulating in their congregation. The result was that some of the Thessalonians (we don't know how many) were becoming "unsettled or alarmed."

What was this false idea that was circulating? Paul does not say much about it, except to mention the rumor "that the day of the Lord has already come." The "day of the Lord" could mean the end times. This involves various signs and events that would culminate in Christ's visible return, the destruction of the universe, and the final judgment. In this understanding of "the day of the Lord," the rumor would have implied that the final signs of the end of the world were taking place and Christ's coming was imminent.

Other commentators, including this writer, consider "day of the Lord" to be the Last Day, when Christ comes visibly to judge the world. In 1 Thessalonians 5:2-4 this is the clear meaning of this expression. Moreover, in the context before us, Paul indicates the subject he is going to address is "the coming of our Lord Jesus Christ and our being gathered to him." Understanding "the day of the Lord" in this manner, the rumor would imply that Christ had already come.

Whatever the exact content of the rumor, its effect on the Thessalonians was clear. Paul had to address himself to it lest its unsettling effect on God's people continue and perhaps spread.

What gave this rumor some status was the added rumor that Paul himself had said the day of the Lord had already come. In his first letter Paul had indeed spent quite a bit of time instructing them about Jesus' "coming" and their "being gathered to him." But Paul categorically denies he had ever said that "the day of the Lord has already come." Though this statement was "supposed to have come" from him, Paul denies ever having spoken such a thing in "some prophecy, report or letter." Anyone who told them Paul was the source of the rumor was deceiving them. Paul urges them not to listen to such deception any longer.

What he says next is, at least at first, quite surprising to us. It was not so surprising to the Thessalonians, because while Paul was with them, he had told them about this more than once. Instead of simply denying the false rumor, Paul launches into a lengthy prophecy about two events that would have to take place before the day of the Lord would come. Since these two things still lay in the future, so did the day of the Lord.

The one thing that would happen is a falling away or a denial. The NIV translation "rebellion" is a possible rendering of the Greek word, which is the same word as our

English *apostasy*. But the following verses, especially verses 10 to 12, indicate that Paul is talking about a denial or desertion from the truth of salvation. In the Old Testament this word referred to unfaithfulness to God or the denial of God. In the only other place where it is used in the New Testament, Acts 1:21, it also refers to a turning away or desertion.

The second event that must take place is the revelation of a "man of sin." The NIV takes the reading "man of lawlessness," which is found in some of the early manuscripts. As the NIV footnote indicates, there are many early manuscripts that read "man of sin." The latter definitely has the stronger evidence. Nevertheless, the NIV's "man of lawlessness" does not introduce anything strange into the New Testament text, because in verses 7 and 8 this man's sin is described as "lawlessness." The sin of lawlessness that would characterize this man is spelled out in more detail later.

He would be particularly responsible for the apostasy, or falling away, because he would be a powerful and influential leader who would presume to take the place of Christ. Thus he is often referred to as the *Anti*christ. Since he tries to take the place of Christ and leads people away from Christ, his fate is sealed. He is "doomed to destruction."

Numerous misinterpretations and speculations have arisen from this prophecy. Many people contend that we cannot know for sure what the fulfillment of this prophecy is. Yet if we take everything that Paul says, neither leaving any of it out nor ignoring or altering the meaning of words, the fulfillment does become clear. This prophecy is fulfilled in the line of men who have served and will serve in the papacy of the Roman Catholic Church.

Perhaps it would help to list all the facts before we study them individually. There are nine points to keep in mind about the apostasy and the Antichrist:

1. The falling away from the truth of salvation would be accompanied by the revelation of the Antichrist, the man of sin.
2. The Antichrist would exalt himself so that he would become the equal of God in the hearts of men.
3. The opposition to Christ was already at work when Paul wrote these words, but God was holding it back from working openly.
4. Eventually God would let it work openly, and this would result in the Antichrist being clearly revealed as an opponent of God.
5. With his Word, Jesus would overthrow the power of the Antichrist.
6. At his second coming, Jesus would completely destroy the Antichrist.
7. The Antichrist would be successful in bringing about the apostasy, because Satan would support him with miracles to mislead many.
8. Satan would also use his power to lead the Antichrist's followers to join the man of sin in denying the truth of salvation.
9. Because of their denial of the truth, God would harden the Antichrist's followers in the delusion that they were on the way to salvation when really they were perishing.

Note in particular two key facts included in all nine points. First, the Antichrist is clearly a religious teacher. He claims to be doing Christ's work, while in fact he is one of the worst opponents Christ would ever have. Second, the span of time of the Antichrist stretches from Paul's time to the end of the world. This includes the Antichrist's rise, time of glory, and the time of continued, though broken, power.

The rise and fall of the Antichrist

⁴He will oppose and will exalt himself over everything that is called God or is worshiped, so that he sets himself up in God's temple, proclaiming himself to be God.

⁵Don't you remember that when I was with you I used to tell you these things? ⁶And now you know what is holding him back, so that he may be revealed at the proper time. ⁷For the secret power of lawlessness is already at work; but the one who now holds it back will continue to do so till he is taken out of the way. ⁸And then the lawless one will be revealed, whom the Lord Jesus will overthrow with the breath of his mouth and destroy by the splendor of his coming.

Paul had introduced the subject of the Antichrist by describing him as a man of sin whose revelation would be accompanied by a falling away from the faith by many. Now he briefly sketches the sin of this man and, in a very broad outline, the history of the Antichrist.

Paul explains a little more fully what the Antichrist would do as the man of sin. His sin is that he not only opposes God but exalts himself above God. The man of sin, man of lawlessness, demands for himself a position above "everything that is called God or is worshiped." The word *worshiped* was a word used in the New Testament time to refer to everyone who held a leading position in the family, government, or religion and was to be highly honored. Paul is saying that the Antichrist exalted himself above these people whom God wants Christians to honor as his representatives. By so opposing God's will, he even sets himself above God!

When the man of sin would succeed in exalting himself in this way, the result would be that he would rule especially in the Christian church as the equal of God himself.

Paul says the man of lawlessness would set himself up in "God's temple." Paul cannot be referring to the temple in

91

Jerusalem. He knew from Jesus' prophecy that it would be destroyed so that "not one stone here will be left on another" (Matthew 24:2). Since Paul's prophecy reveals that the Antichrist would continue his sitting in God's temple until the end of time, he must be thinking of some other temple.

Paul was accustomed to using the term "God's temple" to refer to Christians, especially to Christ's or the Holy Spirit's dwelling in the hearts of Christians by faith. In 2 Corinthians 6:16, for example, Paul declares, "We are the temple of the living God." And in 1 Corinthians 3:16 he says, "Don't you know that you yourselves are God's temple and that God's Spirit lives in you?" Peter expresses a similar thought when he speaks of the Christians forming a "spiritual house" (1 Peter 2:5).

The major result of the Antichrist's exaltation, then, would be that in the Christian church he would tyrannize the hearts of believers by demanding to be recognized as God's equal. The clearest fulfillment of this in the Roman Catholic papacy is the consistent upholding of the principle that the "tradition" (the official teachings of popes and councils) be given equal place with, and in some cases greater authority than, the Word of God. Moreover, the exaltation of the papacy over every one of God's earthly representatives in the family, state, and church was proclaimed by Pope Boniface VIII (1294–1303): "It is altogether necessary to salvation for every human being to be subject to the Roman Pontiff." This proclamation still stands as the official position of the papacy.

Paul reminds the Thessalonians that he had told them about the Antichrist when he was with them. Remember that Paul seems to have been in Thessalonica only a matter of weeks. During this short time he had not been able to instruct them on everything. For instance, in 1 Thessalonians 4:13-18 Paul instructed them about Christ's coming and "those who fall asleep," since the Thessalonians were "ignorant" in this area. The Antichrist was not such a doctrine; they knew about it before Paul wrote. He had shared it with them during his stay in Thessalonica. Obviously, then, this was not a doctrine only for advanced Christian knowledge. And it surely is not to be classed as one of the "problems" of theology and the Bible, as many suggest today. It was and is a matter that concerns every Christian, including those just new to the faith.

Since Paul had instructed them well on this subject, he says that it is a matter of common knowledge among them what was keeping the man of sin from exalting himself already at this time. There was a "proper" or right time according to God's plan to let the man of lawlessness loose. In verse 7 we will come to the statement by Paul that it was a person who was holding the Antichrist back. But here Paul says it was a thing (neuter) holding back the Antichrist. That "thing," which was a matter of common knowledge to the Thessalonians, was the Word of God and the believers' love for that Word. By his Word, Christ maintains his place in the hearts of believers against anyone who would try to displace him. As Paul counsels in Colossians 3:16, "Let the word of Christ dwell in you richly." By believing and sharing that Word, Paul and the Thessalonians were using the "thing" by which the man of sin would be held back. When in later years the love for God's Word would grow cold in the church, then God would allow the Antichrist to come into full bloom and exalt himself in the hearts of people.

Paul warns the Thessalonians that "the secret power of lawlessness is already at work." There were attacks on the truth of the gospel already at this early date. Either shortly before he wrote his letters to the Thessalonians or about the same time, Paul wrote the letter to the Galatians. There he condemned a "gospel" that pretended to be genuine but was not. Soon Paul and the other apostles would have to write many other letters warning against men who were trying to tyrannize the hearts of believers by imposing their own doctrines as the equal of God's Word. Elsewhere Paul warns about "false prophets, deceitful workmen, masquerading as apostles of Christ" (2 Corinthians 11:13). Peter issues a similar warning: "There were also false prophets among the people, just as there will be false teachers among you" (2 Peter 2:1). And John even calls one of them by name: "Diotrephes, who loves to be first, will have nothing to do with us" (3 John 9).

Indeed, Satan was already secretly at work. He was laying the groundwork for the revelation of the Antichrist and for the tyranny that the man of lawlessness would impose upon the Christian church.

The time would come when the "thing"—God's Word and the believers' love of the Word—would no longer hold the Antichrist's power in check. Then, Paul goes on, the one who continued to hold the man of sin back would step out of the way and the "lawless one" would be revealed. The NIV translation "taken out of the way" could be improved upon. The Greek literally says "goes out of the middle," which in English is better translated "steps out of the way" or "leaves the scene."

Who is "the one" who at Paul's time was holding back the revelation of the lawless one? Several interpretations have been suggested. One is that it is the individual Christian, such as each Thessalonian believer. Each loved God's Word and so prevented the Antichrist from getting any hold in his heart. When such Christians "left the scene" and were gradually replaced by others whose love of the Word was lukewarm or cold, then the Antichrist came into full bloom. Another interpretation is that the "one who now holds it back" refers to a gospel preacher such as Paul who eventually would be succeeded by so-called gospel preachers who would proclaim what people's "itching ears want to hear" (2 Timothy 4:3) instead of the truth.

This writer, however, understands this person to be Jesus. Since his ascension Christ has been given the task of ruling over all things for the good of his church. At Paul's time Christ did not permit the Antichrist to blossom, even though his secret power of lawlessness was already at work. But the time would come when Jesus would "step out of the way" and permit the Antichrist to flourish for a while (verse 8) as a judgment on those who still had his Word but no longer followed it faithfully (verses 9-12).

Paul had already explained what the Antichrist's being revealed would mean. The man of sin would oppose and exalt himself over God and all his representatives and rule in the Christian church as God's equal. After this happened, Jesus would step in and "overthrow" the lawless one "with the breath of his mouth." The breath of Jesus' mouth is his Word. "My word," declares God, "goes out from my mouth" (Isaiah 55:11). God's Word held the Antichrist in check, until the Christian church slowly but surely lost its love for that Word. But when the Word was almost totally lost under the accumulated doctrines of the papacy (purgatory, penance, treasury of merits, mediating priesthood, indulgences, asceticism, the ban, condemnation of justification by faith alone), Jesus restored the "breath of his mouth." At the time of Martin Luther and the Reformation, the Lord overthrew the tyranny of the papacy. By the preaching of God's pure Word the gospel was restored. Many heard and believed the truth that they were completely saved by Christ alone, not by subjection to the Pope and his teachings. They were freed from the papacy's tyranny.

Yet the papacy's power was not destroyed. Though many were freed from the rule of the man of sin, many others in their blindness chose to continue under his tyranny. Paul prophesied that though the lawless one would be overthrown by the breath of Jesus' mouth, his destruction would not come until the end of the world. Then Jesus would "destroy [him] by the splendor of his coming."

Satan uses the Antichrist to damn people

⁹**The coming of the lawless one will be in accordance with the work of Satan displayed in all kinds of counterfeit miracles, signs and wonders, ¹⁰and in every sort of evil that deceives those who are perishing. They perish because they refused to love the truth and so be saved. ¹¹For this reason God sends them a powerful delusion so that they will believe the lie ¹²and so that all will be condemned who have not believed the truth but have delighted in wickedness.**

After giving a general description of the sin of the man of lawlessness and a brief overview of his rise and fall, Paul now turns to the apostasy, or falling away, that Satan would cause by the agency of the man of sin.

When the lawless one would exalt himself as God's equal in the church, he would not accomplish this great feat on his own. Satan would be right there using all of his own power as a fallen angel to help the Antichrist reach his zenith. Satan would deceive people into thinking the Antichrist was actually a servant of God.

The devil would help the man of sin by displaying "all kinds of counterfeit miracles, signs and wonders." The adjective *counterfeit* describes these miracles; they are deceptive. Satan would see to it that both real and fake miracles would take place and that the Antichrist would get credit. In this way people would be deceived into following the Antichrist as a man of God, since they did not know that these signs and wonders were done by Satan's power, not God's.

Satan has the power to do real miracles. As a fallen angel he has superhuman, though not almighty, power. The devil even deceives those false teachers whom he helps to do miracles into thinking they are serving Christ. But Jesus says that on the Last Day, when they stand before him and boast of what they have done in his name, they will be rejected! Jesus will not deny that they did the miracles, but he will reject them as evildoers because their power did not come from God. "Many will say to me on that day, 'Lord, Lord, did we not prophesy in your name, and in your name drive out demons and perform many miracles?' Then I will tell them plainly, 'I never knew you. Away from me, you evildoers!'" (Matthew 7:22,23). Scripture warns that we must not be swept away by a religious teacher who does miracles. Rather, we must use God's Word to examine what he teaches. Then we will know whether his power comes from God or whether Satan is doing miracles for him in order to deceive people into believing his false doctrine.

In Roman Catholicism the working of signs, wonders, and miracles by Satan is an integral part of the religious system developed by the papacy. Perhaps the best example is one of the requirements for a person to be declared a saint. Before the pope can declare a new saint, a commission must investigate reports about the person proposed for sainthood. It must establish as true that at least three miracles took place through the prayers of this person.

The whole system of Mary and the saints is an attack on Christ. Scripture teaches that Christ is our only Savior and the only "mediator between God and men" (1 Timothy 2:5). Instead of teaching people to trust in Christ their Savior for the forgiveness of all their sins, the Roman Catholic Church teaches people to look to Mary and the saints for help with their venial sins. Instead of going to Christ their mediator for help in time of need or trouble, people are taught to use

Mary and the saints to get help from God. These errors are greatly aided by the display of miracles, signs, and wonders performed by Satan to assist the Antichrist in his deception.

In addition to the deceiving signs and wonders, Satan does something else for the man of sin to blind people spiritually so they do not know the way of salvation. One of Satan's methods in blinding people to the truth is to make false teachers appear as the most sincere and pious messengers of God's truth. Jesus describes them as wolves "in sheep's clothing" (Matthew 7:15). Satan himself often "masquerades as an angel of light," and so, Paul says, "It is not surprising, then, if his servants masquerade as servants of righteousness" (2 Corinthians 11:14,15). None of the devil's servants will come saying, "Look out for me, I'm going to lead you to hell." Quite the opposite, and this is also true of the Antichrist.

Satan also makes the Antichrist's teaching about salvation seem to be the truth. The expression "in every sort of evil that deceives" indicates that Satan works in every evil way possible to blind people to the fact that following the Antichrist is a way of unrighteousness rather than a way of righteousness.

Those who allow themselves to be deceived in this way are "those who are perishing." In a long continuous line from Paul's day when the "secret power of lawlessness" was already at work until the end of time when Christ will destroy the Antichrist "by the splendor of his coming," Satan has led countless souls to their doom by the error of the man of sin.

These perishing souls have nobody but themselves to blame. Paul says, "They refused to love the truth and so be saved." Before the Antichrist came into bloom, he was held back by the preaching of God's pure Word. Only when Christians turned away from the truth of the Word did Christ let the Antichrist exalt himself. When the man of sin had fully revealed his error and his opposition to God, Christ overthrew him by his Word, "the breath of his mouth." The truth of the gospel was restored to the church. Freedom from the tyranny of the Antichrist was proclaimed. Still, many did not believe the simple and joyful message of salvation by grace alone through Christ alone. Why not? Partly because Satan was working to blind them to this glorious truth, but also because they refused to believe it.

Since they chose to follow the Antichrist rather than "to love the truth and so be saved," God allowed Satan's "delusion" to take firm hold of their hearts. Two results come from this obstinate unbelief. One is that they "believe the lie" of the man of sin. Although the Bible reveals the Antichrist's teaching to be in opposition to the truth of God and although these people read and study that Word, they never see the contradiction. The second result is that they "will be condemned." Though they live in the delusion that the Antichrist is leading them on the way of salvation, they are headed straight for hell. Once again, this is because they "have not believed the truth but have delighted in wickedness."

This is the most terrifying thing about the papacy. In the guise of godliness, it teaches a way of wickedness. Almost all of the teachings that have been added to the Bible in Roman Catholicism in some way or other deny Christ's full and free redemption. They teach instead a form of self-righteousness. Roman Catholicism does indeed urge people to believe in Christ for their forgiveness; but then it also teaches people to do deeds of penance, to attend mass, to pray to God through Mary and the saints, and to suffer in purgatory. The church imposes all these laws so that people add their own supposed good works to what Christ has done.

Scripture says that adding anything to what Christ has done separates completely from Christ and causes a complete loss of God's grace. "You who are trying to be justified by law," writes Paul in Galatians 5:4, "have been alienated from Christ; you have fallen away from grace." This way of self-righteousness is the way of *un*righteousness or wickedness. Our good works and good intentions are never sufficient, because they are always tainted with sin. Only Christ's perfect life can satisfy God, who is perfect and demands perfection.

Self-righteousness, then, is the error that lies at the heart of the apostasy prophesied by Paul. This is the fatal error of the man of sin (the man who leads people to sin rather than to belief), the man of lawlessness (the man who opposes God's will rather than doing it), the Antichrist. It is the error he uses to bring about the apostasy with Satan's help.

This prophecy was not just written by Paul for the Thessalonians. God led the apostle to record it for our instruction too. Paul considered it an essential doctrine for every Christian, even for those new to the faith. So should we. It is an urgent warning to avoid the error of self-righteousness, which causes Christians to fall from their salvation.

In addition to *the* Antichrist, other antichrists continue to plague the church. "As you have heard that the antichrist is coming," declares John, "even now many antichrists have come" (1 John 2:18). All share the common error of which we have been speaking.

We need constantly to guard against their error. We need constantly to warn one another against the Antichrist and all other antichrists who teach a way of salvation other than through Christ alone. We need to pray for one another, as Paul does for the Thessalonians in the next verses, that God would preserve us from self-righteousness and keep us in our Savior.

Paul thanks God that the Thessalonians follow Christ

[13]**But we ought always to thank God for you, brothers loved by the Lord, because from the beginning God chose you to be saved through the sanctifying work of the Spirit and through belief in the truth. [14]He called you to this through our gospel, that you might share in the glory of our Lord Jesus Christ.**

Paul repeats the obligation of thanks he feels toward God that he had earlier expressed in 1:3. There he said he owed a debt of thanks to God for enabling the Thessalonians to grow in faith and love in spite of bitter persecution. Here he expresses thanks for their election from eternity and for their call to faith at the present time.

Moved only by his undeserved love, God had chosen the Thessalonians to be believers. Actually God had carried out this choosing or election even before he created the world. In our comments on 1 Thessalonians 1:4 we had noted how the doctrine of election assures us that our salvation rests in God's wisdom and power rather than in our feeble hands. This choosing by God had one goal in mind, namely, that the Thessalonians might "be saved."

God accomplished this goal by the "sanctifying work of the Spirit." Men can choose to reject the truth, as they do when they follow the Antichrist, but they cannot choose to believe in Christ as their only Savior. This choosing only the Holy Spirit can accomplish by working the miracle of faith in a human heart. "No one can say, 'Jesus is Lord,' except by the Holy Spirit" (1 Corinthians 12:3). By bringing them to trust in Jesus as their Lord, their Savior, the Holy Spirit sanctified or made the Thessalonians holy. As they heard the gospel, the Holy Spirit led them to accept it as true. He led them to believe its message of Jesus' redemption of the world as the only way of salvation.

101

Paul, Silas, and Timothy had had the privilege of bringing this saving gospel to the Thessalonians. They also looked forward to sharing with the Thessalonians the future glory that was their firm possession in Christ.

After speaking of the followers of the Antichrist as believing a lie and being condemned to hell, Paul now speaks of the Thessalonians as believing the truth and looking forward to sharing the glory of Christ. No wonder he felt obligated to thank God on their behalf! Here again Paul stresses that these blessings were theirs only because of what God did. God chose them from eternity. God established the gospel of salvation by sending his Son. God sent Paul to preach this gospel to them. God called them to faith through his Spirit by the preaching of that gospel.

If we believe the truth of Christ and reject the lie of the Antichrist, let us remember this is all God's doing, not ours. And remembering this, we will also feel an obligation. It is the debt of thanks we owe God for his goodness to us.

Paul urges the Thessalonians to stand firm

¹⁵**So then, brothers, stand firm and hold to the teachings we passed on to you, whether by word of mouth or by letter.**

¹⁶**May our Lord Jesus Christ himself and God our Father, who loved us and by his grace gave us eternal encouragement and good hope, ¹⁷encourage your hearts and strengthen you in every good deed and word.**

God had called the Thessalonians to follow Christ and not the Antichrist. This would mean nothing if they failed to stand firm in their faith. As we have seen, the error of the man of sin easily deludes Christians, because Satan himself is hard at work promoting this lie. Therefore Paul urges the Thessalonians, and us, to stand firm. Stand firm against every attack on our faith by the Antichrist or by any other servant of Satan who teaches some form of self-righteousness.

How can we stand firm? This is done, Paul asserts, by holding tightly to those teachings he and the other apostles have "passed on" to us. When Paul uses this expression, he is stressing that none of the thoughts or words he expressed were his own. They came to him from God the Holy Spirit, and Paul merely passed them on to us. To the Corinthians Paul declared, "We speak, not in words taught us by human wisdom but in words taught by the Spirit" (1 Corinthians 2:13). That's why we can "hold" to these teachings with the utmost confidence. We can grab on to them and never let go, for we know they will not fail us. They are God's own words. Strengthened by constantly reading and hearing them we will be able to stand firm.

The Thessalonians had these teachings passed on to them "by word of mouth" as well as "by letter." We have them only by the letters or writings of the apostles, but this really matters very little. How they come to us is far less important than the fact that they are the very words of God "passed on" to us.

Not only does Paul urge the Thessalonians to stand firm in faith, he also prays that their faith may be put into action "in every good deed and word." Standing firm in faith includes more than clinging to God's pure Word as taught in the Bible. It means living that faith. We share the gospel with others. We speak only words that are helpful to our neighbor. We do deeds of kindness to those in need so that they see the love of Christ in all we do.

Our old Adam will work hard to keep us from such words and works. But God will encourage and strengthen us so we can crucify our old Adam and walk in step with the Holy Spirit. How does God do this? Paul's prayer indicates the motivation God uses to accomplish this goal. It is God's love. "When we were God's enemies, we were recon-

103

ciled to him through the death of his Son" (Romans 5:10).
Was there ever greater love than this?

And the Lord "by his grace gave us eternal encouragement and good hope." As an undeserved gracious gift, he
gave us the wonderful blessings of encouragement and
hope. In our earthly trials and tribulations, he supplies us
with encouragement. We can bear our troubles patiently
because we know God will make them serve our eternal
good. And for the future, he holds before us a "good hope."
We enjoy the certainty that after this vale of tears we will
share with our Lord an eternity of joy. Was there ever
greater grace than this?

Who would not be encouraged and strengthened by
such a loving and gracious God? This is our motivation to
do every good deed and speak every good word.

Paul asks for the Thessalonians' prayers and assures them of God's protection

3 Finally, brothers, pray for us that the message of the Lord may spread rapidly and be honored, just as it was with you. ²And pray that we may be delivered from wicked and evil men, for not everyone has faith. ³But the Lord is faithful, and he will strengthen and protect you from the evil one. ⁴We have confidence in the Lord that you are doing and will continue to do the things we command. ⁵May the Lord direct your hearts into God's love and Christ's perseverance.

In closing the section on the Antichrist ("Finally . . ."),
Paul does two things. He solicits the Thessalonians' prayers
for his mission work and assures them of the Lord's protection. In both instances Paul is thinking of the enemies of the
gospel, such as the Antichrist.

The reception of the gospel in Thessalonica was a marvelous event. During Paul's relatively short stay, the Thessalonians had become devoted Christians who lived their faith,

suffered persecution without denying their faith, and spread that faith through all of Greece. Paul wanted the Thessalonians to pray that the gospel might take hold in the same way where he was now working, the large and influential city of Corinth. This city was the gateway to the West as far as mission work was concerned. The establishment of a congregation in Corinth would provide a firm jumping-off point to Rome and to Spain in which Paul longed to spread the name of Christ.

When Paul requests them to "pray . . . that the message . . . may spread rapidly and be honored," his meaning is clear. Paul not only wants the gospel to reach many places, but he also desires that many believe it. When people believe in Jesus as their Savior, they honor him. When people live lives of faith, they bring praise to their Father in heaven. This is what we ask for regularly when we pray, "Hallowed be your name." We are asking God to send the Holy Spirit that we may hallow God's name by believing his Word and by leading holy lives according to it.

Why does Paul need the prayers of the Thessalonians? Because there are many, many people whom Satan uses to oppose his preaching. Paul emphasizes this with a classic understatement: "Not everyone has faith." We Christians know what a treasure we have in Christ. Naturally we expect our fellowmen to want to share in that treasure. But when we try to tell them about this priceless yet free gift, we find most are not interested. We find it difficult to comprehend why everyone doesn't have faith. We learn in sorrow the truth of Jesus' words that his flock will always be a little one. And it will also be hated by the world. "If the world hates you, keep in mind that it hated me first," says Jesus (John 15:18).

This was the trouble Paul faced in Corinth. God had encouraged Paul to preach the gospel boldly in Corinth. In a vision one night, the Lord had told Paul, "Do not be afraid; keep on speaking, do not be silent. For I am with you, and no one is going to attack and harm you, because I have many people in this city" (Acts 18:9,10). Yet there was bitter opposition. And just as in Thessalonica, Jews were among the gospel's worst enemies. Even though God had promised to protect him, Paul asks the Thessalonians to pray further that he, Silas, and Timothy might "be delivered from wicked and evil men."

It's not that Paul doesn't trust God's promise and so feels the need for the Thessalonians' prayers. No, he realizes that their prayers are one way in which God confirms his promise. So in asking them to pray, Paul shows his confidence in the Lord. Someone without faith wouldn't even make such a request.

The term *wicked* has the idea of being "out of place." These were people whose "place" one would expect to be with Christ (the Jews who were God's Old Testament people) but who instead were against him. Thus these people were evil. They served Satan and not Christ. They were part of the "secret power" of the Antichrist that was "already at work" (2:7). Encouraged by the Lord God himself and with the Thessalonians praying for him, Paul was not about to despair because of the opposition he faced.

Furthermore, Paul knew "the Lord is faithful." The Lord who elects and calls to faith and who commissions to preach the gospel in all the world, also promises to be present everywhere with his protection. To this promise, as all the others, Paul knew God would be faithful. In their prayers for Paul, the Thessalonians could appeal to God's own faithfulness.

This was a great assurance for Paul and the Thessalonians. So Paul turns right back to them and declares on the basis of God's faithfulness, "He will strengthen and protect you from the evil one." The evil one is Satan. From whatever evil Satan might throw at the Thessalonians, be it persecution or the error of the Antichrist, the Thessalonians could be sure to escape unharmed spiritually. By the means of grace the Holy Spirit would "strengthen" them in faith. By the mighty angels and his almighty power God would "protect" them from any eternal harm.

Therefore, Paul is confident. He is sure that any report that comes to him will show that the Thessalonians are doing what he had commanded them. He had urged them earlier to "stand firm and hold to the teachings we passed on to you." Paul's confidence that they would do this rested "in the Lord," who had "chosen" the Thessalonians "to be saved." God would continue "the sanctifying work of the Spirit" and "belief in the truth" among them.

Paul's closing prayer asks the Lord to direct their hearts like arrows straight toward "God's love" and "Christ's perseverance." If the thoughts of the Thessalonians were concentrated on God's gracious love in Christ, the error of the Antichrist would have no influence on them. And if their thoughts were focused on the perseverance of Christ in all his suffering because of the "joy set before him" (Hebrews 12:2), it would be a powerful example for them to persevere in their persecution because of the "good hope" set before them.

As we look back on this last portion beginning with 2:13, several things stand out for our special consideration:

1. The Holy Spirit is still working to preserve Christians in the faith and to bring them to glory. Paul's obligation, a debt of thanks to God, is one we share. We keenly feel this debt, because God in his mercy continues his saving work.
2. The gospel is still spreading rapidly and being honored. In Africa, Asia, and South America, souls are being won by the "message of the Lord" that Christian missionaries

proclaim. Since "wicked and evil men" still oppose this message, our missionaries need our prayers as much as ever.

3. The "evil one" is still doing whatever he can to keep us from standing firm and clinging to God's pure Word. We need to pray for one another constantly, that God would "strengthen and protect" all of us and direct our hearts totally to "God's love and Christ's perseverance."

Pray, pray, pray! That's what all three points in this section inspire us to do. And we can do it in the confidence that "the Lord is faithful." He will surely hear and answer these prayers because he has so promised.

What is keeping us from praying? Surely there is reason for prayer. The Antichrist is still strong, though broken in power by the "overthrow" he suffered in the Reformation. Satan is as powerful and cunning as ever. Let the apostle's example and his call to prayer move us to prayer right now.

PART THREE

Disciplining a Brother in the Sin of Idleness
(3:6-18)

Paul urges separation from those who live off others

⁶In the name of the Lord Jesus Christ, we command you, brothers, to keep away from every brother who is idle and does not live according to the teaching you received from us. ⁷For you yourselves know how you ought to follow our example. We were not idle when we were with you, ⁸nor did we eat anyone's food without paying for it. On the contrary, we worked night and day, laboring and toiling so that we would not be a burden to any of you. ⁹We did this, not because we do not have the right to such help, but in order to make ourselves a model for you to follow.

Having discussed the judgment of God and the Antichrist, Paul now comes to the third and final subject of this letter. This was also a matter on which he had taught the Thessalonians previously: work and idleness.

In commenting on his first letter, we noted how Paul had warned the Thessalonians not to become loafers, dependent on others for the necessities of life (1 Thessalonians 4:11,12). He had urged the congregation to admonish such people (1 Thessalonians 5:14). But apparently some didn't accept Paul's instruction or listen to the admonition of their fellow Christians.

Now in the name and by the authority of Jesus, Paul commands the Thessalonians to take action in regard to their unrepentant fellow members. They are to "keep away from every brother who is idle." These idle Christians had been taught what was wrong with their actions. They had

109

been warned that to continue in such a way of life was living in sin. They could not plead ignorance of their sin. Since they refused to repent, the congregation had to take the next step that Jesus said must be taken with an unrepentant brother. Jesus outlined the procedure in Matthew 18:15-17: "If your brother sins against you, go and show him his fault, just between the two of you. If he listens to you, you have won your brother over. But if he will not listen, take one or two others along, so that 'every matter may be established by the testimony of two or three witnesses.' If he refuses to listen to them, tell it to the church; and if he refuses to listen even to the church, treat him as you would a pagan."

To impress on a sinner that his sin excludes him from God's family, the other members of this family are to treat him as an outsider. The purpose of this action is to lead the unrepentant sinner to realize the seriousness of his sin so he repents and is saved rather than continuing on his sinful path to his soul's destruction.

By referring to his own actions when he came to Thessalonica, Paul underscores the fact that those who were idle could not plead ignorance. Not only had Paul taught that idleness is sin, but he had conducted his own life in Thessalonica in a way that made this point clear to all the Thessalonians. He set a working example. He urged all of them to follow it in contrast to the usual habit of Greek men who tried to avoid working with their hands.

Paul said he would have had every right to expect the Thessalonians to supply his bodily needs when he preached the gospel to them. God wants people who are taught his Word to provide a living for their teachers: "Anyone who receives instruction in the word must share all good things with his instructor" (Galatians 6:6). Nevertheless, Paul avoided accepting anything from the Thessalonians. He didn't want to encourage the sin of idleness, which was prevalent in Greek society of that day. He went so far in this that whenever anyone provided a meal for him he insisted on paying for it!

To take care of his needs, Paul worked with his own hands. Most likely he made tents, which according to the book of Acts was a skill he knew. In describing his hard work and long hours, Paul repeats almost verbatim what he had said in 1 Thessalonians 2:9: "Surely you remember, brothers, our toil and hardship; we worked night and day in order not to be a burden to anyone while we preached the gospel of God to you." This repetition also underscores the point that his own example was well known to them.

Idleness is contrary to Christ's will

¹⁰**For even when we were with you, we gave you this rule: "If a man will not work, he shall not eat."**

¹¹**We hear that some among you are idle. They are not busy; they are busybodies. ¹²Such people we command and urge in the Lord Jesus Christ to settle down and earn the bread they eat. ¹³And as for you, brothers, never tire of doing what is right.**

When Paul had been with them, he had given them a very simple rule to remember. If anyone doesn't want to work but simply wants to live off others, the Thessalonians were to let him go without food. God did not want his command that we love our neighbors as ourselves to be abused by loafers. Nor does God desire Christians to encourage the sin of loafing by providing food for those living in this sin.

Much has been made of this "rule" stated by Paul. Some have used it to attack the system of labor unions we have in our country. Others have used it to say that the United States' welfare system is wrong. We must be careful, however, to read the rule carefully. It does not say, "If a man doesn't work," but, "If a man will not work." The Greek word for "will not" points to an attitude in the person. If this point is clear, we can apply the rule properly.

Labor unions and the welfare system were not established to foster a sinful attitude of idleness and living off others. It is true that they have been abused by some who have this attitude. As Christian citizens we will speak out against such abuses and try to change them. Labor unions and the welfare system do serve God-pleasing purposes. They prevent the fleecing of workers by greedy employers. They correct working conditions harmful to the human body, which is God's creation. They assist people who cannot work because there is none available or because they are too disabled or ill.

Once again, the key point is that Paul addresses himself to an attitude. We are not to condone or foster a lazy attitude by giving support to a person given to this sin. In our society we can try to change laws or institutions that we know are wrong in this regard. We may not have much success in changing the attitude of idleness in people who are unbelievers. But if we know of a fellow believer who is caught up in this sin, we have an obligation of love to call him to repentance.

Paul fulfills this obligation by speaking to the unrepentant. Paul had heard there were some loafers in the Thessalonian congregation. Making a play on words, he says that instead of being "busy" like they should be, they are merely "busybodies." Instead of leading a "quiet life" at home and "minding their own business," they spent their time poking their noses into other people's lives and gossiping.

Just as he had commanded the congregation to stand aloof from these idlers, Paul now commands these people to stop their sinning. Their idleness was not a trifling matter. By their sin they were actually denying their Savior! For it was Christ's will that they provide for their own needs. And by their sin they lost "the respect of outsiders" (1 Thessalonians 4:12) and brought shame on the Savior whose name they bore as Christians.

To those involved in this sin, the apostle adds an encouragement to do what is right. They were Christians who Paul sincerely hoped would turn from their wrong. The NIV's "settle down and earn" and the KJV's "work with quietness" both relay Paul's thought. They point to the two things repentance calls for here: the people were to (1) stop being busybodies and (2) begin using their hands to provide their own living. Then they would no longer be dependent on others for food. They would eat the bread they themselves had earned.

Turning again to the faithful Thessalonians, Paul urges them not to be influenced by the sin of the idle and "never tire of doing what is right." To see someone loafing and living off others while we struggle hard to make a living can be demoralizing. We quickly grow tired of hard work. The devil whispers in our ears, "Why work so hard? Look at those other people. They're not working at all, and they're living even better than you!" But Paul whispers in our other ears, "Don't envy those idlers. They're under God's judgment, because they're living in sin. Listen to your Savior, who loves you and died for you. His will is that you live quiet lives, mind your own business, and provide for your own needs as much as possible. Do what is right. You will please your Lord and glorify his name before your neighbors."

Discipline should seek to win back a brother

¹⁴If anyone does not obey our instruction in this letter, take special note of him. Do not associate with him, in order that

he may feel ashamed. ¹⁵Yet do not regard him as an enemy, but warn him as a brother.

The rule Paul cited earlier said that anyone who didn't want to work should not be given anything to eat. Paul had also given the command "to keep away from every brother who is idle" (3:6). Now, in his final words on the subject, Paul adds some further instruction on how this separation was to be carried out in order to accomplish the spiritual goal of calling an idle person to repentance.

The idlers had no excuse for continuing in their sin. While in Thessalonica, Paul had set an example by his hard work. He had also instructed them. In his first letter he had told them, "Warn those who are idle" (1 Thessalonians 5:14). In his second letter, he again broached the subject. If, after all this, anyone still persisted in his sinful attitude about loafing, the congregation must take action. It was to serve notice to the lazy person that because he was unrepentant he could no longer be considered a Christian.

To impress this on the lazy person, all of the members of the congregation were to avoid any kind of association with him. According to Paul's words in 1 Corinthians chapter 5, this went beyond excluding him from the Lord's Supper; it also meant not even eating with him. Paul taught that the unrepentant sinner—whatever his sin—must be avoided: "You must not associate with anyone who calls himself a brother but is sexually immoral or greedy, an idolater or a slanderer, a drunkard or a swindler. With such a man do not even eat" (1 Corinthians 5:11). We cannot share the Lord's Supper with an impenitent sinner because Christ gives us his body and blood to assure us of forgiveness. But if a man is unrepentant, he has no forgiveness. Giving him the Lord's Supper would tell him something that isn't true and might well encourage him to continue to be unrepentant. To deny him the Lord's Supper is telling him what is true, namely, that he has no forgiveness. God often uses this refusal to give him Christ's body and blood to bring such a sinner to repentance. Furthermore, when the rest of the members of the congregation refuse to have any association with the unrepentant sinner, this also helps to say to the individual that his sin is serious and he is lost because of it.

To socialize with an unrepentant person, then, while the congregation is disciplining him in an attempt to bring him to repentance may undermine what the congregation is trying to do. For example, if I dine at his house or play a game of tennis with him as usual, my actions can easily be understood by him to say that while the congregation may think his sin is serious, I don't. Thus I would encourage him to think more lightly of his sin than if I were to decline his invitation with a gentle, yet firm, statement of why association with him would be wrong on my part at this time.

The 1 Corinthians passage goes on to say that we will not necessarily disassociate ourselves from people of the world who live in unrepentant sin. "What business is it of mine to judge those outside the church? Are you not to judge those inside? God will judge those outside. 'Expel the wicked man from among you'" (1 Corinthians 5:12,13). We would have to leave the world to completely avoid every unbeliever! No, the disassociation is from a brother who knows Christ but whom Satan has gotten to deny Christ by continuing unrepentant in a sin.

We want to preach a powerful law sermon to him by our disassociation so that, as Paul says, "he may feel ashamed." That our motive is one of love Paul now underscores. He carefully instructs the Thessalonians in regard to the frame of mind in which they are to deal with their unrepentant brother. Paul urges them not to think of him in any way "as an enemy." They were not to have hostile feelings toward him that would lead them to say "Good riddance!" if he left and never came back to the congregation.

Rather, the Thessalonians were to "warn him as a brother." What they said to him about his sin and their explanation of why they were disassociating themselves from him were to be carefully planned and spoken in a gentle, pleading, loving way. The message to be conveyed was that Christ loved him and had died for his sins but that this sin of idleness in which he persisted was a denial of that Savior's love. That denial would damn him. And that damning result troubled his fellow Christians who wanted him to be saved rather than lost eternally. By not associating with him the congregation would issue a loving warning. It was a warning such as a person who knows of serious danger ahead on a road will give to someone whose life will be threatened by continuing down that road.

This is an important passage for explaining the purpose of church discipline and how to carry it out in love. It also establishes a number of truths about the disassociation or denial of fellowship we must practice over against a persistent sinner: (1) This is done not only when someone denies basic truths of our Christian faith, such as the person or work of Christ, but also when he denies our Savior's will in any way. This includes what might seem to some to be such an insignificant matter as loafing. (2) Every member of the congregation is to take care in any daily contact with a person under discipline that he does not undermine the congregation's purpose. Members dare not soften the church's law message to the unrepentant sinner. (3) The first step in dealing with such a person is *not* to disassociate from him. Rather, as Paul did, we will patiently instruct (his visit to Thessalonica), warn (1 Thessalonians), and warn again (2 Thessalonians). Then if a person does not repent, we will disassociate. Even this will be done in the frame of mind that we are dealing with a brother, not an enemy.

Carrying out church discipline as God wants requires the right mix of patience and firmness. This mix will not be hard to come by, if it is truly love for a brother's endangered soul that guides all we say and do.

Closing prayer, greeting, benediction

¹⁶Now may the Lord of peace himself give you peace at all times and in every way. The Lord be with all of you.

¹⁷I, Paul, write this greeting in my own hand, which is the distinguishing mark in all my letters. This is how I write.

¹⁸The grace of our Lord Jesus Christ be with you all.

The persecution the Thessalonians faced, the threat of the Antichrist, the necessity of practicing discipline—the three subjects on which Paul has spoken in this letter must have been disquieting for these believers. Paul's final prayer asks that God would give his peace to the Thessalonians in spite of all these disturbing developments. The peace for which he asks is the peace God established between himself and sinful mankind by Christ's death on the cross. He requests this blessing for them "at all times." Paul prays there will be no break in the stream of peace to them, whether times were good or bad, happy or sad, difficult or smooth. He also asks this blessing for them "in every way," that is, both spiritually and physically. Knowing that their souls rested in Christ's peace, the Thessalonians could live with confidence. Their bodily sufferings, their daily tasks, the pleasant experiences in life all would be tempered by the peace they had in Christ.

In asking that the Lord would be with all the Thessalonians, Paul is asking what God already promised to do. Nevertheless, he prays this for the Thessalonians, because he wants to remind them that he is concerned with each and every one of them. He wants them to be assured of God's abiding presence and to take comfort in that fact.

Paul emphasizes that he is writing the greeting here at the end of this letter in his own handwriting. Does this imply that someone else wrote the rest of the letter and Paul dictated it? Most likely. The Thessalonians had been unsettled by a rumor started by a letter that Paul supposedly wrote. Consequently, he assures them this letter was not forged but genuine. He adds that this was his regular practice, by which they could easily distinguish any forged letters from those really written by him. They could compare any other supposed letters from him with the genuine handwriting they had in this one, because he says, "This is how I write."

This letter closes, as did the first one, with the familiar benediction Paul used. He assures them that their Lord, who is the promised Prophet, Priest, and King (Christ) and the Savior (Jesus), will continue to shower his free and undeserved love on all of them.

We have come to the end of our study of Saint Paul's letters to the Thessalonians. Very little is known about the early Christians in Thessalonica other than what we learn in these two letters. What we do know inspires us. It makes us thankful the Holy Spirit led Paul to write to the Thessalonians.

As we've seen, this congregation had its shortcomings. The people were unclear about whether Christians who died would ever live in heaven or not. They were too easily unsettled and alarmed when they heard a rumor that the day of the Lord had already come. They did have idle members whom they had to discipline. But for the most part the Thessalonians serve as models for us, just as Paul said they did for all the believers in Greece. "You became a model to all the believers in Macedonia and Achaia" (1 Thessalonians 1:7).

These model Christians had kept the faith in spite of severe persecution. They spread the gospel as far as they could. They loved their faithful pastor. They clung to God's Word. They lived to please God and to love one another. They eagerly awaited the Lord's return. They admonished weak or erring brothers. They were constantly growing in faith and love. They held to the teachings passed on to them by the apostles. These were the Thessalonians' strengths that we noted as we studied the two letters. We thank God for all these blessings he poured out on the Thessalonian Christians!

We pray that the Lord would bless us in the same way. As we read these words penned more than 1,900 years ago, may the Spirit also work in us, preserve us in the faith to our end, and give us a share in the glory of our Lord Jesus Christ.

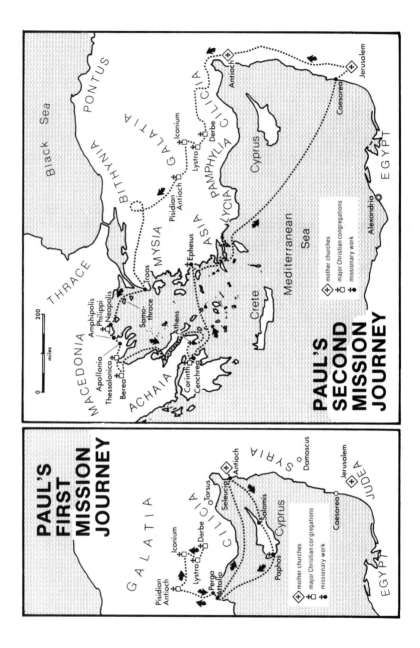

PAUL'S
SECOND
MISSION
JOURNEY

⊕ mother churches
✝□ major Christian congregations
✝● missionary work

PAUL'S
FIRST
MISSION
JOURNEY

⊕ mother churches
✝□ major Christian congregations
✝● missionary work

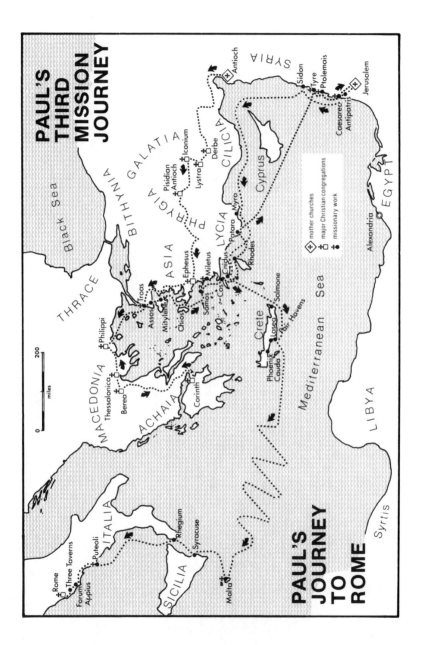

PAUL'S THIRD MISSION JOURNEY

PAUL'S JOURNEY TO ROME

mother churches
major Christian congregations
missionary work

0   200
miles

Black Sea

THRACE

MACEDONIA
Thessalonica
Berea
Philippi

ACHAIA
Corinth

BITHYNIA

GALATIA

PHRYGIA
Pisidian
Antioch
Iconium
Lystra
Derbe

ASIA
Troas
Assos
Mitylene
Chios
Samos
Ephesus
Miletus
Cnidus
Cos
Rhodes

LYCIA
Patara
Myra

CILICIA
Antioch
SYRIA
Sidon
Tyre
Ptolemais
Caesarea
Antipatris
Jerusalem

Cyprus

Crete
Phoenix
Cauda
Lasea
Salmone
Fair Havens

Mediterranean Sea

EGYPT
Alexandria

LIBYA

Syrtis

ITALIA
Rome
Three Taverns
Forum Appius
Puteoli
Rhegium
Syracuse

SICILIA

Malta